MAN GOING HIS OWN WAY

By Bernard Chapin

This book is dedicated to the Glory of God. AMDG. *Soli Deo Gloria!*

Terrestrial thanks goes to Davis Aurini, Matthew Forney, and Aaron Clarey. Thank you so much for your advice.

This book created with direct support from Joseph S. C. MacDonald, Vince Rozyczko DVM, Eddie Rico, Kaspar, Jonathan Paul Hendey, Alan MacNeil, Gerald Ciesla, Ruth, Doug Mitchell, Phil Dickerson, and Kyle A. Durston. Without my audience I would be nothing.

Table of Contents

The purpose of this book is to reveal my own example of why I choose to Go My Own Way. I also want to discuss the negative trends I have observed which brought me to this point. I speak without bitterness or anger. As always, with my writing or videos, I seek to entertain as well as instruct. Several of the recollected incidents in these pages had me giggling as I typed them. I hope to have the same effect on you, my reader.

The Chapin Theory of Female Crypsis: *Whenever a woman is presented with the reality the women and men differ in occasionally unfavorable ways, they will reflexively emit two responses. The first is to deny the veracity of the statement and the second is to claim that "men do it too!"*

Chapter 1: The Long Farewell

I cannot and will not recant anything, for to go against conscience is neither right nor safe. Here I stand, I can do no other, so help me God.
—Martin Luther

"REAL MAN" societal definition: an ignorant conformist with millions of manipulation receptors existent and open for binding with the multivariate requests of any female he comes across. Thinks of other men as being either competitors or random evil doers.

Now I am non-directional. I have both nothing and everything. Yesterday is lost but the only thing to do is march forward. I have chosen my own way. That is my deeper purpose.

The present is not what I anticipated. I, like so many others, expected to be married and have children by my current age. Yet what I wanted is not what is. I accept my situation… completely.

I also did not foresee the difficulties we face unique to these times.

I am content with reality. I will die a single man.

The decision was never close. The distance between my idea of what a wife should be and the actual characteristics presented by "modern women" are too vast. I am now a Man Going His Own Way (MGTOW)[1] and will be one for the rest of my life.

What I try to do in the pages that follow is tell my own story and describe the events that caused me to make this decision. Perhaps they apply to you as well, and my perspective is one that many men in the Manosphere will appreciate.

My title was purposefully selected. I chose not to call the book MGTOW as it has already been used by others. Had I employed the acronym, this work could have been viewed as my attempt to tell the history of the movement (or non-movement as the case seems to be). I am not the right person for this task, and, frankly, such a book would make for a boring read.

Moreover, I am a controversial person within the MGTOW online community due to past conflicts I have had with a couple of other video content creators. Some of their loyal supporters have misinterpreted these personal disagreements as an indication that I was against Men Going Their Own Way. Nothing could be further from the truth.

Unlike many an internet avatar and uploader of videos whose identities are hidden, I have complete skin in the game. I am very much alone. I use my real name online and have done so for 13 years. There is no place for me to hide.

A simple google search eliminates me from many forms of employment. In some fields, there is not an opinion that I could express on any societal topic which would be accepted. At this point, I go my own way by definition. I have no choice.

My ethics collide with those of our age. I value learning, study, and the contemplative life. In 2016 these are deemed anti-social traits.

The media and our universities promote guilt, shame, and ignorance among the population. Young people are thoroughly miseducated today. They are taught that the history of America is embodied by slavery and segregation. They are encouraged to take no pride in their nation and have no interest in history. They are asked to regard themselves as the starting point of civilization. This is false. The last few decades have marked the beginning of our slide into barbarism.

Little is known of the past even that which occurred during my own life time. Last year I used to ask young people if they had heard of "East Germany." They hadn't. This year I've asked if the "Soviet Union" means anything to them. Only half recognize the name, and even those individuals could not tell me much about it.

How better to dupe a population than to withhold the necessary knowledge by which they can understand the past?

A cohort that knows nothing about history will decide our future elections based on guilt, slogans, emoticons, group affiliation, and fabricated self-righteousness.

I point these truths out on my Youtube channel, and also ridicule politically correct behavior. This makes me a serious enemy of the establishment. Already, on two separate occasions, there were attempts to have my employment terminated. I was reported to the local police who were asked to evaluate whether I was "a threat." What kind of threat could I be?

The harridans behind this concern-ruse could not logically defend their own positions any more than they could read Clausewitz. Better to purge me from their sight than face their own stupidity.

Our foes do not believe in argumentation and debate. Those are tools of the oppressor in their eyes despite the fact that they spend their time oppressing us. Our society is thoroughly misandric. Every man is guilty of something, and, should he question the dominance of women, then he practically is a felon. Not viewing females as my superior renders me "sexist" today.

Women, the ornate sex, are faced with no such tribulations. For them, it is not the same. Women *need* to conform. Whatever becomes the dominant mindset—in this case cultural Marxism[2]—they will then become its bullyboy enforcer. Women are the ultimate adapters to changing times. Twenty years ago they all thought that marriage was between a man and a woman. Now they will fanatically suggest that you are anti-gay should you say anything resembling it.

You cannot ask a Philistine to make intellectual distinctions, and Philistines are the only thing our culture creates nowadays thanks to Hollywood. It is practically impossible to alter these people. Brains contaminated by reality TV cease to be brains after a short period of time.

Large swaths of the female population were indoctrinated in college to believe idiocies like my sister being born good while I was born evil due to the nature of our differing genitalia. They confuse discussions of gays and transsexuals with "politics." They are amoral creatures and do not really believe in much of anything except advancing their own interests.

Conformity is the real "c-word" when it comes to women. They obey every trend. Fashion is a perfect example. Gay male fashion designers dictate what clothes they should wear even though the tycoons suspiciously only hire models who look like little boys. They refuse to see through the scam. Instead, normal males are then blamed for anorexia and bulimia under the fiction that we are attracted to women who look as if they never went through puberty.

Similarly, the scripts for the television show *Sex and the City* were written by male homosexuals.[3] I could tell by watching the program that what was depicted was not female sexuality at all. Yet most women detected nothing phony about it. The show still has cult status among many patsies who seemingly believe that the characters onscreen are their "friends."

Women comply with all of the risible, loathsome tenets of political correctness including the hoax that PC is not political. The opposite of the Marxist cant is political rightism, but people refuse to make this connection.

I still recall the shocking experience of several women telling me that political correctness is simply kindness and good manners. They honestly believed it and regarded my counter-arguments as being a conspiracy theory.

When someone is that anti-intellectual there is little hope of improving them. They are not open to education. One is tempted to sell such persons a nearby bridge or highway, but they would probably be unable to buy them because all their money was already "invested" in vacation trips instead.

Personally, I am glad to have been born a man even with all the female privilege that I miss out on. Embracing principle over trend is not easy, but it's the only way.

There are plenty of other guys like me. Most of them are smart enough not to use their real names. More and more the fellows who identify themselves publicly are being fired from their jobs for questioning the propaganda of the left. The next step will be imprisonment for heretics. I firmly believe this is the direction in which we are headed.

Winston Churchill was right when he said, "The fascists of the future will be called anti-fascists." Already we see this happening in the "anti-fa" dragoons who run around beating people up for simply opposing unlimited immigration. I have no doubt they will eventually come for us.

Merely expressing a view that was non-controversial thirty years ago—such as *viva la difference*—is enough to put you in the crosshairs of the elites who so tragically mismanage western civilization at present.

Each year the expectations grow greater and greater. PC never stops metastasizing. Tolerance used to be the goal. Then came acceptance. Now it is celebration. It's not enough to know about the gay pride parade. You are expected to be down there at the side of the road in order to "support them." Have fun.

Our speech is constantly being modified and structured without our permission. Many of these attempts to correct are merely done to put us on the defensive and give others the ability to dominate us.

One must give the Oprah head-nod whenever he is asked to confirm the anti-American drivel known as multiculturalism, feminism, statism, affirmative action, diversity, and that only some of our lives matter.

There will be no head nods from me. My defamers can go to hell.

I am a thought criminal in the greater eyes of society, but so is any man who takes up the defense of his fellow men. We are told to advance the cause of women and to let their needs be our own. Never. I advance the cause of freedom and truth. I will go my own way. **I am going my own way.**

I wage intellectual war, but I am a happy (and often giggling) warrior. I encourage you to be the same. At 46, I am still excited about every day. I am not a father or a husband, but I am still a man.

In hindsight, I believe I was as choosey as a woman when it came to mate selection. Long-term, it was a most productive strategy as I did not hold onto an Edsel for 20 years. This limited my short-term production, however.

No one feels sorry for those older women who partied their twenties and thirties away without planning for the future. Then, after they rode the Esmay Carousel for 20 years, they suddenly want to get married. That is both a comedy and a tragedy, but MGTOW, at least, won't pop the question to any wayward dirigibles.

We mock these older women often, indeed I still do, but their lives bear little resemblance to my own. They made really bad decisions, and now they want to blame others for their ignorance and stupidity. Asking someone like me to marry one of them is absurd. You cannot forge a domestic future out of toxic waste.

Over the course of my "career," and, despite hundreds of dates with hundreds of women, I never found more than four who I wanted to marry. Of the four, one of them I did marry, and to another I got engaged. The other two were dismissed by my own hand. I was glad to be rid of them at the time, and I still am. I have no regrets.

Sometimes I wish I had children, but I never wish I had a wife. I will die a free and proud man despite not having any heirs. My "issue" will be the continued viability of western civilization.

Most of my friends on the internet, do not believe in God. I am fortunate to think differently. I live for a higher purpose. I use the tools that I was given and I am grateful to possess them.

I am a passionate man. There are few subjects upon which I am moderate. Either I have no opinions or I have serious opinions. The things I like, I often love. I am attached to a great many things in this world, and without question nearly all of them are masculine endeavors or activities.

Despite age and its accompanying lower testosterone levels, there is almost nothing female about me. I have never believed in that flummery about men having a "feminine side" which is nothing but newspeak.

I want to follow my passions. I don't want to focus on "stuff" or status or entertainment. I want to create and produce. Many women would find my life "boring."

Well, if you are bored then you are probably boring. I prefer a minimalist lifestyle to a rat race.

I find that a great many men have their interests dumbed-down once they enter into a relationship. Sandman has talked about this much on his Youtube channel.

That happened to my friend Bones. After marrying an average looking vulgarian, his essence completely changed. He used to be an abstract, philosophical guy, but soon he was working 60 hours a week. He was harried every minute of the day.

Soon Bones stopped reading literature and even listening to good music. Bones started listened to *her* music. Mommy was his new DJ. I recall hopping into his car one time and hearing him sing an Eagle-Eye Cherry song. Bones had memorized the lyrics. It was demoralizing to observe. To focus on lyrics that moronic is a sign of mental deterioration, yet syrup pop became his new love. What a thing upon which to squander a prodigious memory.

The lowest moment in our 15 year friendship came when he asked me, "How can you live on so little money?"

"I don't have a wife," I said. I then stared at him for about ten seconds. Who was this fool? What had my oldest friend turned into? No man talks that way to another man. It was as if his spirit had been hijacked by the soul of his vapid wife.

I refuse to compromise my passions. I won't allow a Sturbannfuhrer to usurp the space between my ears. I want to be free. It's easy for me. My choice is between liberty or some woman in her 40s...which means there is not a real choice at all.

Another reason to go your own way is that the government has taken the side of women in relationships. After you say "I do" you also consent to let the civic authorities run your life.

Since the 1970s, marital rape emerged as a new doctrine wherein all a devious wife has to do is have sex with her husband. Then she can call 911. This results in an automatic reversal of the burden of proof. The physical evidence against her man is already swimming inside of her. It would then be up to the husband to demonstrate that he had her permission before the act occurred.

Marriage jeopardizes a man's entire existence today.

Child support payments are mandated yet a woman's proper accounting of that money is not. She can spend the cash on whatever she likes.

Actor Jon Cryer's wife asked him to pay her $89,000 a month[4] despite the fact that Cryer had full-time custody of their child.[5] In the end, his ex-wife had to settle for a *paltry* $8,000 a month. What she needed to spend the money on is unknown. Her argument seemed to be "he makes so much more than me." Her demands appeared to have little to do with their child.

The courts have made marriage a masochistic endeavor for men. If everything works out...then it works out. Congratulations. If it does not, you could end up like Britain's Peter Morris.

The judge in his divorce case awarded his ex-wife every cent he possessed. This case was made more unusual by the fact that the judge went even further than that. He insisted that Mr. Morris pay his ex-wife an additional 77,000 pounds for "unpaid maintenance and other debts."[6] He left the proceedings with nothing and additional debt more expensive than my house. If that was not rape I do not know what rape is.

Gynocentrism, with its inherent misandry, has become the religion of the western world. What do we owe women? There is an easy answer: **everything**. Not just our wealth and earnings (that's obvious) but also our physical well-being. We are expected to defend even unknown females if they are endangered. I say nuts to that.

If you are not dear or known to me then I owe you absolutely nothing. *You've come a long way baby![7]* Now you will fight for yourself. You do not need me or any other man. You are strong and independent. If you win, congratulations! If you lose, I will be happy to commemorate your existence with a lively story at the bar.

Feminists now sell t-shirts and drink out of mugs reading "Male Tears" and "I Bathe in Male Tears." This reveals the lack of compassion and empathy that many women have for men. Both the media and our universities bait men continuously despite their ubiquitous narrative of "women are peasants and men are nobles." What a lie.

What kind of oppressed person taunts their oppressor? There are no historical examples of it. Russian citizens never harassed officers of the KGB. No Jew molested a storm trooper, and zero Armenians tormented the Turks. That stuff never happens. The claim that women are at a disadvantage in society cannot bear scrutiny of any kind. The arguments against it are simple and obvious. That's why they shout "misogynist" when you disagree with them.

Affirmative action is nothing more than a government program that allows women to be hired and promoted over men. It's sick and it's evil. Men have nothing to do with female vocational outcomes, but the fib must be perpetuated so the program can be justified.

Disparate outcome does not prove discrimination. That I would fail in the NFL or NBA does not mean that anyone plotted against me. I never had the talent to be in either league. When women struggle, men are blamed. Why? When they succeed our society attributes that achievement to a woman's superior abilities and temperament.[8] All of it is mumbo-jumbo.

When men make known their knowledge of this sham we are branded misogynists, sexists or Neanderthals. All of these names are flimflam. Increasingly, the term sexism has morphed from being synonymous with discrimination into "criticizing a woman publicly or privately for her behavior." That's not sexism. It's a pro-social outcome in my opinion.

What they do not want is for men to organize and talk back. They have no logical basis for their claims. It's all feelz and subterfuge.

Our prospects would be good in terms of exposing the deception were it not for the fact that most men are white knights. These males feel righteous about defending a woman...any woman. Even the ones whose villainy is conspicuous. Men are raised to defend women and never ourselves.

The fact is, I was raised an egalitarian. I grew up thinking of women as my equal and that is the way I treated them. I thought they would be considerate, loyal, hard-working, and honest. That is the way I am after all. Yet I was subjected to criticism throughout my youth, whereas, most women never are. They truly believe they are "special."

People make excuses for female misbehavior which helps to massively degrade their personalities and their character.

Socrates said that "the unexamined life is not worth living." Women today are living proof that his is the minority view. Many of them seem set on acting out the fictional existences of characters that they see on a multitude of jejune television shows.[9]

Johnny Q-Bob summed up my problem precisely back in 2000. He was my best friend at the time. He had seen me pick up countless women, go on dates with them, and heard many a tale. Johnny said,

> *Stop talking to these people like they're men. Stop expecting them to be honorable. Just have sex with them and stop thinking about "marriage material." Have some fun!*

I should have taken that advice seriously long ago.

While I still treat women as my equal, I have practically no expectations out of them.

All MGTOW are alienated from the outer world in some form or another even if they do not share my political views. Man was not meant to be isolated …but we are. It is clarity of perception—*perspicax*—that has made us so.

I cannot revise the past. It's MGTOW forever for me now.

Chapter 2: Blood on the Blade

No son, never. The blood stays on the blade. One day you'll understand.
                    —Priest Vallon, *Gangs of New York*

We dreamed of her and compared our dreams
But that was all that I ever tasted
                    —Billy Bragg

My awareness of the opposite sex came early…frighteningly early. An often told family story concerned the beach in La Jolla, California.

I was two and following around a four-year-old girl named Coco. I think that was my first memory. I ran into her house—to do what?—and saw her father laughing at me. What happened after that was unknown but my relatives giggled about it repeatedly in the 70s.

I was a most promising lad.

The future rolled forth in a predictable direction.

In kindergarten the mother of the best looking girl in our class happened to be a friend of my mom's. I know I did not think of her sexually but did regard her as being really cute. One day she came over for lunch. We sat and watched *Underdog* together (my choice). She reached over and we held hands as I ate a tuna fish sandwich. What she ate I have forgotten.

The next day in school she said little to me. How disquieting. It was all downhill from there until I was an eighth grader. Hand holding surpassed any achievement I had for the next eight years. Rejection was what I experienced most in my youth although a lot of the time I just wasn't paying attention to the opposite sex.

By the time I started to understand females and had improved my ability to attract them, they began to lose their luster. This outcome will be discussed in detail in the fourth chapter.

At age nine though, I do remember having a particularly wicked dream about Suzanne Sommers which greatly confused me. I had her picture on the wall from the Sunday *TV Guide*. She was on the cover. I was aware of her being "hot" but did not really know what that meant. My dreams did though. We were entwined engaging in something that was absolutely nuts. I knew about "sex" but only had an ethereal understanding of it. I used to love seeing her on *Three's Company*. After that night I knew why.

When I was in fifth grade my family used to go to this rinky-dink restaurant in Troy, Michigan. Its name I cannot visualize now. My dad loved the place because it was cheap and also did not serve alcohol. He quit drinking in 1979 and could not handle being in any of his old haunts. Therefore, we drove to the place on a weekly basis.

I remember sitting there and watching the "Miracle on Ice" in 1980. I stood up and jumped on the booth's upholstery as our guys scored. Whenever I hear the chant "USA! USA!" I still think of the first time that I heard it.

One day they had a new waitress who was probably 18 or 19 but seemed worlds older than I. I thought her beyond sexy. She wore a shirt with a zipper on it. It was unzipped down about 5 inches from her neck. Her breasts were ripe and visible.

Those things were *rolling folders*. I could not believe it. When she asked for my order I began stammering in response. Every time I saw her the testosterone flowed and I could look at little else. On the days when she was not working I wanted to go home and come back the next day instead.

The pattern of my life was set though in the sixth grade. Through this story we can see that the child really is the father of the man.

In Mr. Francis's social studies class, one day the best looking girl in school, Elsie, got caught passing a note to another girl by our Sherpa. Mr. Francis was a former World War II bombardier. We loved the guy. We often tried to get him to tell us tales, but it was rare that he would mention his time in the South Pacific.

Mr. Francis was the coolest guy I knew next to my Uncle Harry. My uncle flew 20 missions over Tokyo. Harry gave me his wings as a reward for my interest in his achievements. I wanted to hear everything, and, unlike Mr. Francis, my uncle loved to rehash the past. I eventually lost his wings though and I still feel shame over it to this day.

Anyway, Elsie had tried to throw "a note" across the room and did so clumsily. I saw it happen with my peripheral vision. "Notes" were things that girls wrote enabling them to talk all day when talk was forbidden. Mr. Francis thought this activity counter-productive. I agree with him, but our views would be labeled as "hate" today. Grown women still write these notes when they cannot openly talk, but now we call it "texting."

Mr. Francis pointed to the paper on the ground and said, "Bernard, give me the note."

Elsie turned around, imploring me to give it to her instead. She said, "Bernard, give it to me!"

I looked at Mr. Francis and then at Elsie. I got up and handed the note to my liege. I did not look at Elsie as I back sat down.

Elsie was fortunate. Mr. Francis ripped the note to shreds immediately. Another teacher, Mr. Spencer, took a different tack. He used to read the notes aloud in a sing-song voice. He thus humiliated the girl in the process. We all laughed including the female students.

In 2016, Mr. Spencer would immediately be fired and all the male students would be tried as accomplices to patriarchy. The female students would be congratulated for having survived His Darkness. They would probably receive presidential medals too. Perhaps a movement would form around them. The busted girl would be expected to commit suicide accordingly so that a new victim group could form around her corpse. She could be a Horst Wessel...a Horst Wessel of their own.

Why though did I sell Elsie out? What about my white knight gene? I am afraid that I was born with one that functions erratically. That is why I got involved in men's rights and will remain a part of the Manosphere until they remove me forcibly from the premises.

Yes, Elsie was really cute and "hot" in my sixth grade eyes. That I followed the teacher's orders is surprising. The reason that I did so was that while I knew Elsie, Elsie certainly did not know me. She never once looked in my direction or spoke my name before that day. I was a piece of lint in her eyes. Selling her out was appropriate and a correct form of social justice.

I remain proud of that story. I salute the 11-year-old me. It foreshadowed the guy in his twenties who would ask girls at bars "what's my name?" after they asked for free drinks. If they did not know it (which they never did) I'd laugh and say "what kind of sucker would I be to buy you something when you don't even know my name?"[10]

At age 11, I was thinking big picture while everyone else was fantasizing about Donkey Kong and Space Invaders. I was a no status male but at least I wasn't a chump.

Throughout those ugly, vicious, middle school years, I remained a geeky guy with glasses and a bushy haircut. I was neither short nor tall, fat nor thin. I was a blur. I was also a blur to myself. I had no powers of self-reflection, but after sixth grade I comprehended that I was a nobody.

I was attracted to several girls but none of them noticed me. I was not the lowest guy on the status hierarchy, but I certainly was in the bottom quartile. Mostly this was due to my being a nerd who did not know what fashion was.

Then, one day in sixth grade, someone made fun of me for wearing Toughskins jeans. Toughskins is a Sears brand for children. I thought they were cool clothes as they had patches on the knees. To me, this indicated my athleticism. I needed those things! I was sliding in every direction and diving for every ball. Couldn't they see that? No, what everyone saw was that I was a loser.

I woke up. I needed to change. Rather than get cool toys for my birthday as I always had done, I asked my mom if she would buy me some Izod shirts and some Levis jeans. The stupid alligator logo was the only shirt the kids at school wore. I was at the age where I cared what everyone else thought. I wanted to be a member of the club. She spent 80 bucks for three Izods and two pairs of jeans (kid sizes and 80s prices).

I then proceeded to wear those items until the threads evaporated.

At Christmas, I got Nikes and a non-Wal-Mart coat. Asking for clothes as presents was a pattern that continued with my parents until I graduated from college. I tried to build a wardrobe but kept growing out of stuff. I tried to wear the tight clothes anyway. People made fun of me for looking like a hillbilly.

One day in 8th grade the high school wrestling coach came to see all of the prospects. He singled me out and told me that I was already earmarked as a starter for him in the varsity division at 98 pounds. He said this would only be possible if I got stronger. He said that without more upper body strength I would "never make it."

I believed him. I started doing 100 pushups and 100 sit-ups each night. Thus began my interest in lifting weights and my desire to workout has yet to be extinguished.

Now, as an adult, I spend very little of my income on clothes. I did not care in 6th grade about that nonsense and I still do not care now. Wearing clean, unstained attire is my only priority. I have more t-shirts and hats than I have months left on the calendar. Who knows where they all came from? Brands and labels are irrelevant, but that was not true in seventh grade. I was still in conformity mode. I wanted girls to like me…but they didn't. I was not even an also-ran in their eyes.

In junior high, I had very little contact with the opposite sex. The girls had a different gym teacher and we stopped talking when they arrived late to the bus stop. Guys who had girlfriends were admired. Yet guys who had friends that were female were ostracized.

To this day, if a fellow tells me that his best friend is a woman I look at him askew and stop listening to what he says. I wouldn't trust a man (sic) like that with a bottle cap. He's either a sissy, a chump or mentally delayed. There can be no other explanation! Fuck him.

Girls at school were like grizzly bears on television; seen but never experienced. We played football in the neighborhood every day after school, and during the winter we played Dungeons & Dragons obsessively. I knew of no females who shared either of my interests.

The level of hostility amongst middle schoolers in the 80s was very high. Adults were seldom around. It was like being in the Yukon. My first rejection came involuntary. A girl sat next to me in science class. She wore a red Derby (that was our school name) jumpsuit. I could not see all of it from where I sat so I asked her what her number was.

She turned and spat, "There's no fucking way I'm giving you my number."

Shocked, I muttered, "Your number on the team?"

"Oh, 17." Then she looked back at the teacher.

My next interaction with a female came in band class. I was the number two chair for saxophone, and the number one chair was absolutely gorgeous. She was sterling. I used to salivate/stare at her as we practiced. She, of course, never said a word to me. To say I had a crush on her was an understatement.

We were members of the same swim club. To my surprise, one day she said that she saw me playing tennis there and wanted to know if I would play her. I cheerfully agreed. Sweet! This was like a date.

I showed up early, but, like Jimmy in *Goodfellas*, she showed up even earlier. I gave her my A game. That was the only game I had at age 12. I did not comprehend "half-speed." I bounced about like a lynx and narrowly won 6-4. I wanted to play another set. She didn't.

I was magnanimous in victory. Her serve was better than mine so I complimented her on it, and asked if she would teach me how to serve better. That statement was the best my limited social skills could muster.

No dice. She was pissed. She refused my request and never wanted to play me again. In retrospect, I think she wanted to smoke a boy at a sport. At 5'0" and 95 pounds I seemed a good candidate. It didn't work out for her, but I enjoyed being in her presence anyway.

After that I thought we were cool and that she was a "friend." Wrong. When

I talked to her in band class she said nothing back. I don't remember ever hearing her voice again until I was a high school junior. In AP History class she whispered to me out of nowhere, "what's Chernobyl?"

Unfortunately, I yet to become the loving gentle man I am today. I laughed in her face. "You don't know what Chernobyl is? That's all that's been in the news for the past three months. How fucking dumb are you?"

That was my revenge for her refusal to be my tennis partner I guess.

The summer before high school I spent all of my spare hours at the swim club or riding my bike around town. My father just started letting me mow the lawn, but, as of yet, I did not have any other customers in the neighborhood. We used to play shark in the diving end of the pool after it closed at 8 pm. It was a flurry of activity for 60 minutes. We had to avoid the hands of whoever was in the middle. A very attractive girl wearing a swim cap played with me quite often.

I never considered her as an option. I assumed she was out of my league. She went to the local catholic school and was not aware of my low status at Derby. I wore glasses back then but always took them off when I swam. Further, all the pushups and sit-ups made me look well-built in comparison to my peers. One day she grabbed me as I was walking out and said, "See you here tomorrow night."

"Yeah." Hot damn!

I meant to go the next day, but my parents made me go see my aunt at the hospital. A week later she was there and acted like she did not know who I was. I had no idea how to remedy the situation. It was beyond my skillset to go up to her and explain that my mom and dad had packed me off to Westland for the night. I saw her years later at Hershel's. She did not remember me at all.

Freshmen year at Birmingham Seaholm High School was like nothing I had ever seen previously. I fell in love with most of the juniors and seniors by the start of the second week. I do not remember much from my classes that year, but to this day I still recall one of the hottest girls in my history class. Her name was Maura. She sat in front of me and one day walked in with a pair of white see-through slacks. Maura had flowered underwear on underneath them. They were totally visible to the naked eye. I fixated on their pattern for the entire hour looking just below the pages of my book in order to stare. My Lord!

That I was a wrestler meant nothing. I was ripped steel. I could bench press 140 pounds when I only weighed 98 pounds. I was a letterman. I even went to states—where I got manhandled. But didn't all of that mean something? Nope. I was still a flunky. Nothing had changed.

The day school ended in 1984 we celebrated by having a game of baseball at a neighboring elementary school. There were probably 15 of us there. Usually, I did not pitch but that day I did. A ball was hit directly at my face. I instinctually covered up my eyes with my glove and ended up catching the ball in the process. I acted like it was standard. He was out. Several of the guys stopped the game to come over and pat me on the back.

About two hours into the game, five girls came out of the woods. They were in our class. I knew all of them by name but that was it. They were wobbling and laughing hysterically. I wondered what they were laughing at. Surely we weren't that bad!

The five girls began stumbling into the infield. One of the middling ones in terms of appearance (about a 6 out of 10) came up to the pitcher's mound. She put her arm around me and started kissing me on the lips and forehead. I was thoroughly freaked out!

I had fantasized about so many girls sexually by then…but not her. She was not in the Betamax. I did not know what to do. I gave no reaction. I stood inert like a bureaucrat. I let her kiss me. I imagine the other girls were doing the same thing to my peers. I cannot be sure though because my attention was solidly affixed to her. A few minutes passed and then they left.

Afterwards nobody wanted to follow them except for me.

Why not I wondered.

I was told they were "burnouts."

Which meant what?

I asked my friend, "So they were smoking cigarettes?"

"No, you moron." He answered. "Marijuana. Couldn't you tell they were high?"

I couldn't. "High? What's that?"

Needless to say none of the girls acted like they remembered the incident when we saw them again. Two years later, the girl's father was my literature teacher. I wisely made no comment to him about his daughter.

We started drinking in tenth grade. I was the first out of the crew from my middle school to use alcohol regularly. This was precipitated by my making friends with two guys a year older than me in speech class. One of them was named Don. He became one of my best friends. He had a killer set up in his basement.

Don was the only guy I knew whose parents were divorced. His dad was seldom over, and, when he was, they were "friends." The rest of us lived in fear of our fathers. We did our homework and did not receive detentions. Not Don. Thinking back, he really seemed like he came from a broken home. Don was clearly damaged by his parents' divorce.

Despite my youth, I could tell that his mother was a flibbertigibbet. She did not work and the well-off father bankrolled the whole clan. Don was physically a man already. He was a stud while I looked like one of the kids yelling in the hallway on *Square Pegs*. His "room" was their basement. It was a shrine to liquor and heavy metal.

We all used to wear jean jackets adorned with heavy metal buttons. I was the lone sellout. Mine included Billy Idol and INXS buttons as well. Don had a huge liquor cabinet that his single mother never bothered to investigate or even ask to open. I recall fondly having two shots of Drambuie or Irish Mist and bouncing around on his trampoline quite often on the weekends.

It was a new group of friends. All of them had gone to the rival middle school, but Don liked me so I was accepted. There were about six of us in all.

I remember that one of the guys—the nicest of them—had a sister named Ingrid. She belonged in a beauty pageant. Everyone stopped to pay homage to her. We were all enthralled with her grandeur. Surprisingly, she had no idea how perfect she was. Ingrid was an 8th grader and she was the first girl I really knew personally. She was coy and fun but a sterile object in my mind. Two years younger than me was jailbait so I never thought of her as someone to ask out. I have no idea what ever happened to her, but, by the time I was a senior, she had become Ms. Popularity. We seldom spoke. Ah, but to have known her when she was younger.

We usually drank at Don's house on Friday nights and then went walking around the Birmingham neighborhoods. No girls were involved but that was not by choice. We watched movies and listened to rock 'n' roll.

My other friends could not believe I had come up with such an awesome "connect." I was the guy to talk to if you needed anything. Don had a fake ID and I used to get him to buy liquor for the others although I made no profit from the transactions. We spent most of sophomore year drinking and roaming around in the dark. Literally and figuratively.

Soon I would discover that alcohol had a powerful influence on my ability to function with women. It would stay an integral part of my social life for the next twenty years. It gave me courage and also made an introverted man appear extroverted.

There was one incident from that period. Don had a big sister named Millicent. She was about 6'1" and we used to refer to her as "Moose" behind her back. When I was a sophomore she was a senior. All of her friends were good looking even though Moose was not. We considered this a fortuitous circumstance and used to swoop around like mayflies whenever her friends were over. We were enthused.

One Saturday, when their mom was on vacation somewhere, we slept over at Don's house. We started drinking at 6 pm. The girls did too in another part of the home. Three or four of us were heavily sedated in the front room when two of the girls wandered in around 9. We were watching *The Outsiders* on HBO.

Don—for reasons I could not fathom at the time—stood up and began spanking semi-hard the best looking of them. He chased her about the house. She yelled happily as he did so.

Girl 2 ignored this. She sat on the couch next to me. I looked up at her. She did not look back. I would have given her a 6.5 out of 10. I was about 5'5" and 135 pounds at the time. I still looked like a boy though. She reeked of wine coolers.

I got back to watching the movie. She suddenly leaned over me and put me in a headlock, jerking me back and forth. The other guys started laughing and cheering, encouraging her to pin me even though I was already lying on my back. I did not know what to do. I remember saying something like, "Hey, I'm on the wrestling team." Well, it didn't look like that as I couldn't budge her.

My lips were right next to hers and I started kissing her. She kissed me back. She freed my arms and they started roving. This probably lasted for thirty seconds. My friends were transfixed as if they were watching a forbidden late night movie on Cinemax.

Suddenly…the girl vanished. She scampered off to the other side of the house where it was pitch black. I looked at the TV and my friends. One of them said, "What the hell is wrong with you? Chase after her."

Awoken, I did just that. I almost cracked my head on the stairwell. When I got to the porch I saw her on one of the wicker couches. I still didn't know what to do. I sat by her feet for a minute and was not sure how to proceed. She entwined me with her legs and we started kissing again. This time it lasted for twenty minutes. I did not see them but I think my friends came over to watch the show.

Then Moose came down and turned on the lights. She laughed at her friend and said, "I'm going to tell everyone what you were doing with this little kid." They then went upstairs to her room to pass out.

I tried to sleep myself but was too excited. I kept looking upward and wishing the girl was back down with us. She was fully developed and I was still about two years from manhood. No matter, I felt like a total stud.

When we got to school on Monday the girl passed me several times and acted like she did not see me. I was young and green. I figured she really hadn't seen me. In the afternoon, I approached her at her locker. I tried talking to her but she would not look in my direction. I had no idea what happened. She never did speak or acknowledge me again, but eventually I understood that she felt humiliated for making out with a sophomore. It was a setback…but I felt like I was on the come.

By my junior year, I had a few similar experiences. A couple of girls would not acknowledge me during the school day after kissing me at some party I attended but was not invited to. Everyone got drunk pretty easy back then. Despite my light weight, I noticed that I didn't. I thought I was cool for having a tolerance. I wasn't. It was an early introduction to genetics. At the time, I thanked God for my Irish and Russian heritage. Now I'm not so sure that's something for which to be grateful.

A couple of redneck brothers named Concannon moved into our district accidentally my junior year. They were from rural Florida. The youngest sat in front of me in Latin class. I became part of their squad. I used to go out with them to McDonalds for lunch where I would buy two 49 cent hamburgers and a glass of water. I still remember the price. It was back when campuses were open. There were no helicopter teachers and the students were free range. I grew up in a great era compared to the kids of today.

We used to love going to Burger King or McDonalds for lunch even though we seldom had more than two dollars on hand at any particular time. We went there strictly to see the presence of girls from the local catholic school, Marian. They were celebrities. I remember walking in there at 12 pm and seeing rows of them at tables in their tartan skirts. It was like attending a fashion show. I felt as if I was seeing the world!

The Concannons proved to be magnificent allies. They had no grudge against anyone because they had just moved into the area. They destroyed social boundaries. They did not know cool people from uncool people. The brothers were not just friends. They were more like heroes. On the weekends they would hear about parties and we would simply show up at them. Invitations we never received. Had I gone by myself I would have been tossed out. Yet the brothers were so jovial and spontaneous the elites were never sure what to do with them. We were seldom refused.

I would accompany them on weekend nights to their father's fitness club and then we would go…wherever. I remember standing there in front of the mirror at the "racquet club" and combing my hair with Vitalis. I would then spray Aqua Velva all over my chest. I thought this a mature thing to go. Then we would head out.

There were many attractive girls at those events and I would often find myself hanging out with one them at some point in the night if only for a few minutes. I always had a buyer lined up for alcohol. The film *Superbad* correctly depicts how hard it was to obtain spirits, and some people would seek me out as if I were a dealer.

I had Don as a purchaser since sophomore year, but also added a punker who lived at the end of my road. He was 23 and gave me a lot of advice. I wish I knew what happened to him, but I can no longer remember his first name. For some reason he always bought us Michelob Dark. I would be seen smuggling in 12 packs of it into parties. I was well-received.

I was only successful with the girls I met for fleeting increments of time. My chances were never good, but they definitely improved if the girl did not know me. Even though I had been in the district since third grade, I was sometimes confused for being a member of an unpredictable southern horde.

Was I a Concannon? Sadly no.

I remember a freshman female who followed me around a bit junior year. She was a fan…the only fan I had. I would sometimes meet her in the park and we would walk around downtown Birmingham kissing. I only saw her in public. Her parents were always home, and French kissing was about as far as I ever got. That was fine with me. She confused me with being a successful older man.

Several humorous incidents occurred my junior year. One that I will recount came when I ran across a girl I knew from science class at a party. Her face was a 5 and her butt was a 10 which meant that I was completely taken with her. She was pretty lit and very receptive. I stood next to her in someone's rec room and soon I had my arm around her. We were by the French doors and I was being a Klingon. I couldn't stop. Touching her was a dopamine highway. She laughed as I did so. She wanted to be worshiped. I was fit to order.

A senior who was a white knight came up to me and asked her if I was *bothering* her. She giggled and I said no. Savior guy did not buy it. He said, "Let's go outside."

I let him walk outside and only followed after he was at the end of the deck. I wasn't afraid of him. He was bigger than me but made of butter.

"What?" I asked.

"Leave the lady alone."

"What the fuck are you talking about you're not going out with her."

"Well, leave her alone you little punk."

"Fuck you man." I stood with my back to the door hoping he'd lunge at me and embed his head in the glass.

He didn't. He waved me aside and walked in; straight to the keg. I strolled back to the girl and kept up my roving hands act. She didn't know where we had gone to, and luckily didn't inquire about the fight that we didn't have.

Yet nothing endured. The girls seldom gave me their phone numbers and whenever they did they didn't call me back. I was just another goof. I loved the film *Sixteen Candles*, but Anthony Michael Hall's character hit a little too close to home.

I believed that nothing was ever going to work for me at that high school. I wanted a girlfriend and I wanted to lose my virginity. Hope and change were coming.

Chapter 3: Actual History

The force that through the green fuse drives the flower
Drives my green age…
                                        —Dylan Thomas

Youth is easily deceived because it is quick to hope.
                                        —Aristotle

My early history with women, as presented in the last chapter, was pretty pedestrian. I was a square and never an alpha anything. My first "relationship" officially occurred when I was 16-years-old. I remember the day perfectly. I was a junior at Birmingham Seaholm High School.

I was still a dork, but, at that point, I had gained enough muscle to deter bullies. That was about all I had going for me. People stopped insulting me randomly which I saw as a positive development. I had a letter jacket as a freshman which brought me countless enemies. By junior year though, most of those guys had already graduated.

My first two girlfriends cast a lengthy shadow on my future due to their (relative) civility and high levels of intelligence.

As far as mental stability goes, they were exceedingly normal. There were a great many opportunities for my college girlfriend to have stalked me or created bizarre amounts of drama, but she never did. I honestly never met a psycho until I was 23.

While most of the girls I dated in my twenties were better looking specimens, I never felt comfortable psychologically with the women I met after college. They were aliens. The first two girls were more like kin. For the most part, those relationships were humane.

In a way the first two ruined me. Dealing with roller coaster females for the next twenty years never fully satisfied after the support I knew as a lad. All the promiscuity, drugs, drinking, and laziness unnerved me. None of that was encountered early on.

They were also feminine women. They were not dudes. There was no spitting, leg hair, cursing or any of the male imitation behaviors that one finds so often present in today's regressive woman.

They were literary and affectionate. I kept thinking that there had to be more women out there like them, but I quickly discovered that most of their kind get married very early. Thus, they never become part of the reusables market.

Did I make a mistake in passing them up? No. I have little nostalgia. Yet I definitely would have been more pleased with what I received later on had I not known either of them in the first place.

I met my inaugural girlfriend one night in the spring of 1986. My friend Joe invited me to a pool party. It was put on by some ridiculous organization he was a part of called "Hugs Not Drugs."

It was all about kids doing things for fun that did not involve drinking. Getting buzzed and exercising were about the only activities I excelled at. I had been sousing for two years and the walls of my bedroom were covered with alcohol advertisements. My parents failed to make the connection between loving a topic and actually engaging in it. I did both.

Drinking took away most of my fears with women. Without it, I would have been lost. This only ended when I became part of the men's movement. My approach anxiety disappeared. With it, I also lost any sense that women were my superior.

Yet in 1986, "approach anxiety" was only the beginning of what I had. It was more like complete terror. As I mentioned previously, I knew few girls personally. I did not talk to them on the phone and I had none of them as friends. They acted like they were not interested in me. I completely believed them. I was not sure what it was that I lacked. I felt unworthy. In their presence, I acted like a serf.

The scene had been set about a week earlier. One day I went out to lunch with my friend, Richton. He had a legendary AMC Gremlin that he bought used, *very used*. He feared it's breaking down on the way to school even though he lived only about a mile away.

On the drive Richton said, "Bern, you could have seriously done some damage at our school, man. You could have been a producer."

"Richton, don't rub it in. You don't think I try?"

"You try, but you need to close the deal and get a girlfriend. Just something that will turn serious…serious enough if you know what I mean."

I knew what he meant. He was referring to my virginity. I needed to get rid of it. I was in full agreement. We went to Burger King to look at the skirts of the Marian girls. It was always a good time.

On the afternoon of the Hugs Not Drugs party, I walked over to my friend Joe's house. We drove his father's green MG convertible all over town. Joe's father was a lawyer with lots of money and his basement looked like a recreated 50s diner. I never wanted to leave and I loved the jukebox.

Eventually we departed and got back into the MG. From there we drove to a private home in Bloomfield Hills. I felt like a subverter and a fifth columnist. I should have been doing advertisements for the spirits industry.

Without liquid fortitude I was incapable of doing anything with women. Yet Joe had raved so much about the talent at these parties that I had to ante up and go. I was not disappointed.

When we arrived, there were about 30 attractive women there. The guys…I did not notice. We immediately went to the pool. Joe introduced me to two girls who stood at the side of it, and soon we decided to go swimming. One of them had long curly brown hair and a magnificent body. Her name was Sylvia. She looked Portuguese, a slim goddess you would expect to see in Lisbon. We spoke very little. I ripped off my ocean pacific shirt and jumped in.

The pool was crowded. From the water I saw Sylvia strip down to her bathing suit which was all white. It was a one piecer cut very high at the hips. "My God," I thought. "I have never seen anything like that." Sylvia looked like a *Sports Illustrated* model. I concluded, "Don't even think about it. That girl is flawless."

My self-worth was low. Her grandeur intimidated me, but so many guys were splashing us with water it was hard to be nervous.

I looked far better than the competition. My male peers did not lift weights at all. Sylvia started gripping me after a few minutes. I held her back. We got out of the water and did not let go of each other until after midnight.

I ate and drank nothing the whole night. I could not get my head out of Sylvia's locks. We made out by the property fence for six hours. Joe was seated next to us kissing another girl. That seems odd but it was not unusual in high school. I got her number. I felt like I had won a Porsche.

We started talking all the time on the phone. Our first date took place on a Friday night. I took her to see Alan Alda's *Sweet Liberty*. The movie was terrible but we kissed the entire time. Her body was like iron. It was the first time I realized how attractive a woman's stomach could be. Hers was sex itself.

We left the theater and I found an isolated subdivision. We then parked the car. We messed around a little bit but eventually I took her home.

The relationship skyrocketed from there. I saw her for seven months.

The pattern of the first night was repeated on the rest of our dates. We used to go to the movies or Denny's. Then I would park the car in some rich subdivision where the houses were set far off the road. I would climb on top of her in the passenger seat and before we knew it midnight struck. I had to take her home.

Sylvia was a track star and went to a rival high school. She was unaware that I was a low status male at my own school. Sylvia said she was not one of the popular kids, but I doubt that her freshman year she had ever been threatened repeatedly with being taped into a locker (in the manner I was).

We had some things in common. We both listened to alternative rock. We were both fit and athletic. We also shared disdain for our own high schools and how stuck up the people were.

We both lost our virginity on the same day in July of 1986…at the same time and location. Her parents were at work but we were both off for summer vacation. I did not have to work at Long John Silvers until 4 pm. I drove my Mercury Lynx over there at around 11. The action was unusual as I wore two condoms (honestly). It was electric and I did not really know exactly what happened.

Despite doubling up, it was over quick! There was blood and a lot of it. Luckily, none of it was mine. I still feared that I had knocked her up. I obsessed about it for a couple of weeks, but that did not stop us from doing it again and again for the rest of the summer.

Overall, Sylvia was a great experience for me. She was easy time and very calm. There were no scenes. She was incredibly low maintenance. Unfortunately, I could not appreciate her. She was the first girl I ever went out. I had met no princesses yet so I did not know how good I had it. A pity.

Sylvia never said too much. I don't recall many details about her personality. She once told me that I may have been more intelligent, but that she was far more complex. I agreed but never witnessed any evidence of complexity.

When we spoke about topics other than "us" we talked about books and film. We used to see movies at the Maple Art Theatre in Bloomfield Hills. She appeared to enjoy them, but made few comments. With books, the only ones she knew were the ones she read for school. We would go to Borders together and she never seemed to be interested in anything.

In the conventional sense though, Sylvia was a mover and a shaker. She got As and Bs in all of her classes. She got into her first choice of colleges. Sylvia was going places.

Did I love her? I thought I did. I was definitely infatuated…for a while. I did not understand love in the least, but I wanted to be around her all the time. After the second date, we both said that we "loved" one other. We said it constantly thereafter. I suppose such utterances meant very little.

My feelings never approached the heights that they did for my college girlfriend though. When we broke up in November I was not devastated. There did not seem to be much to her. I did most of the talking. If I were with her today I suppose long hours would pass with neither of us uttering a sound.

Sylvia and I never spoke again. In my twenties, I heard from a guy I knew who relayed that she had blamed me for ruining her life. What? How? Her life was not ruined in any way that I could detect. What the hell was she talking about?

She is still Joe's friend on Facebook. Her profile is public. She posted lots of pictures. When I look at her face I do not recognize or remember it. Sylvia's white bathing suit and the raven curly hair are all I can visualize. Sylvia still has that hair. Sadly though, if I passed her on the street I wouldn't know who she was.

She weighs even less today than she did when I knew her. Gone are the plump curves. Her body is sinewy and defined. She shows her physique off in athletic shots on Facebook. I am not sure why though. There now appears to be little female about it.

Sylvia was always insecure about her appearance. Now she has become thinner than a blade of grass. Perhaps this was done out of a desire to get back at her male admirers.

She got married a few years ago, but wasn't when I first opened her profile. Sylvia wrote about that in her Facebook intro: "I have a boyfriend but he is not on Facebook so I cannot identify him." Seeing that really made me laugh out loud. The female insecurity about being "with someone" was stamped in bold at the top of her profile page.

I bear her no ill will. Good luck to her.

I may have loved Sylvia, but Maja was the first girl who took over my life. My feelings for my college girlfriend escalated to a point that I would wish them upon no other man.

What follows is a humiliating story. Yet I feel obligated to tell it just in case anyone accuses me of glossing over my history. It is a case of enflamed passion, psychological arson, and nearly attempted murder. I wish I could spin it differently.

In college, Maja was a freshman when I was a sophomore. John Carroll was a small school and I basically knew what everyone who lived on campus looked like.

I recall only seeing Maja once though before she joined the debate team in January of 1989. In the fall, I was walking through the library and happened to notice a girl curiously smiling in a study carrel. She looked to be having a great time in there memorizing terms.

I took note of her due to her unique appearance. I thought she looked Indian. Like a Brahmin, but I really did not know any Indians at the time and could not have specified. She was attractive, but so was just about every other freshman before the age of obesity began.

The debate office was very small. There was evidence everywhere and only three people could be seated at once. I was sitting in one of the three chairs with the top varsity guys going over a strict liability case that was all the rage.

Then Maja walked in. Her smile was something. She wanted to know, "Is this where I go if I want to join the debate team?"

I pointed down the hallway towards the boss's office. The two other guys were far more desperate and geeky than I. They wanted to know her name and introduce themselves.

They stood up. I remained seated. I thought they were scaring her off. I was embarrassed so I pointed again to the good doctor's lair. She noticed my hand motion and got out of there before the two of them leeched onto her like eels.

I had little contact with her that semester. I was hanging out with Grande, Granger, and Harris. We knew few females. It was college so there were strikes here and there. Nothing too thrilling. None of us had fake IDs so we could not get into bars. The parties we attended were mostly with artsy girls who resented physical exercise. I was not into it.

Basically, I was living the same androgenic existence I had in high school. There was this girl from Syracuse I dug who I would see every other weekend at debate events. We hooked up once, but, unlike me, she was in high demand back home. She did not take my attentions seriously. I gave up on it.

Maja was around the debate office a little that spring. I only talked to her once. I asked her if she was Indian. This was not the right question to ask.

"With a name like Maja you think I'm an Indian?"

I knew I had offended her but did not mean too.

"Well...gee...I have never heard that name before. What are you then?"

"Polish."

"And you're mixed with what?"

She raised her voice. "I'm not mixed with anything. Both of my parents are Polish."

I did not even have the decency to apologize. I had no social skills. When people got mad at me my defense was to get mad at them right back. Juvenile. Fortunately, I soon matured. Many women never do. I have seen them react in the same manner as adults 100,000 times.

What I did not realize then was that Maja was sensitive about her dark features. She looked about as stereotypically Polish as I do aborigine. Without realizing it I had stumbled onto a great strategy. I had *negged* her. This made her notice me. Her irritation in no way turned her off.

We then had a debate party in late April at the coach's house. It just was the swinging event you would expect! All of just sort of talked a lot and drank cheap wine. The graduate assistants got high around back…standard.

I said hello to Maja. She ignored me. Maja was being conspicuously fake-nice to everyone there…except for me. This pattern continued throughout our entire relationship. It's a real contrast with how I am. I am respectful to everyone but I save my best stuff for my favorite people. I have a great deal of difficulty not treating the people I like well. If you're in good with me you're always in good with me. If I consider you a friend you'll always know it.

It turned out that Maja's mother lived five miles from my parents. She had attended the local catholic girl's school, Marian, in Birmingham. I told her about the Burger King and all the girls there wearing their tartan skirts. She was one of them. I felt like I was meeting a celebrity. I gushed about how cool I thought it was to go in there and observe. We loved seeing them.

This did not impress her. "Why did you *love* seeing the Marian girls so much?"

"Well, you know…I'm a guy…and…"

Eventually, I got her number. I asked if she wanted to meet me at the local Denny's over the summer. She said okay. She did not have much to do over those months aside from working for her uncle.

I got back home though and my social life exploded.

Lynch had all sorts of things going on in Ann Arbor. I got hired the next week at the now defunct Arbor Drugs, but I had the first weekend off. I spent three days up there in a row. We partied the whole time. I hooked up with few women at John Carroll, but I was on fire with Rob in Ann Arbor. I was walking tall.

I called Maja the next weekend. She only had Saturday afternoon open so I took it. We ordered fries with ranch dressing as everyone did in our social circle when at Denny's. She smoked heavily.

We talked all afternoon. I saw her as a friend. I addressed her like one of the guys. I told her about hooking up with random women in Ann Arbor. Hell, I was bragging. I could not resist. I had no social skills. The previous weekend greatly relieved me. I had feared that sex was going to be something that only other people did.

Maja was petrified by my story. She told me that I was a male slut and a person of low moral fiber.

What the hell was that? Only adults had spoken to me in that manner. I did not have the sense to alter my conversation for my audience yet. I think she thought this was supposed to be our first date, but I felt it was just two college buddies doing the hang. I laughed at her pronouncement.

I still did not get it. I was thick. I said, "Man, you should have been there!"

We met the next week at Denny's again. Then we walked around my favorite place in the state of Michigan: The Cranbrook Educational Community. It is paradise for introverts.

When I got home from college each summer Cranbrook was practically abandoned. The fields were open, so was the lake and the surrounding manicured woods. I fucking loved that place. You were supposed to pay on the side, but we always snuck in around the back. We never got kicked out.

When I went there with Maja we looked damned respectable as a couple. I toured the place constantly until the day I moved to Illinois in 1995. To this day, when I think of "home" I think of Cranbrook.

Our second rendezvous seemed more like a date. Even I noticed. I also started looking at her body. It was exquisite. I could not tell then but it was obvious (in retrospect) that she liked me. By the boathouse at Cranbrook, the sacred boathouse, we had our first kiss. The kisses never stopped thereafter. It may have been pheromones but I could not get my lips off of her.

We began talking all the time. We went out every night after my shift was over at the drugstore. She was always home with her family. Even if I only had a couple of hours I still drove over there to see her.

Her mother hated me. In the course of the relationship I even told her that I would consider converting to Catholicism. Why not? I went to mass at John Carroll, and the catholic churches were more majestic than any of the protestant churches I had been in. My parents would not have cared. They were both atheists.

Maja's mom was not interested. "Why wasn't he a catholic in the first place?"

It soon became apparent though—to everyone who knew me—that I had fallen in love with Maja. This was not a crush. I was destroyed. I wanted to be with her every minute of the day.

Maja was not content to have only one smoker in the relationship. She was the most powerful advertisement Phillip Morris ever had. Maja, although she denied it later, used to try to get me to smoke with her. I said no…for a while. Soon I gave in.

We walked all over Bloomfield Hills and Troy late at night smoking and making out together. This lasted for two months until the fall semester began. I would park on the side of the road behind the same isolated homes that I did with Sylvia. I would round the bases with her in the car with the lights turned off.

I only reached home plate in late July. Maja continued to call me a whore because I had been with two other women before her. She said she basically was not a virgin due to a guy she had fallen in love with in high school. I made no comment. I did not know what "basically" meant.

I smuggled her into my bedroom after my parents had gone to South Haven for the week. My elderly uncle was asleep. We spent the night there. In my mind it was not sex. We made love. It hurt me to type that last sentence but it was true. I was completely enamored with her. When we were done I felt wet. In fact, I was drenched. Confused, I turned on the light. There was blood all over my bed.

I whispered frantically, "I thought you weren't a virgin."

"Well, I fooled around with the guy sophomore year but I guess he only sort of put it in." Sort of meaning "not at all" I guess.

"Maja this is nuts. What am I going to do? It's like I killed you or something. These sheets are covered."

"Well wash them."

"What will my uncle say? He'll think I'm Manson."

We ended up putting a blanket over the sheets and slept on top of them. Lots of blood, no foul.

Maja, and my ridiculous attachment to her, had severely changed me. I was no longer recognizable. I stopped calling Lynch or going to Ann Arbor. I no longer called anybody except Maja. I used to make fun of guys like the one I had turned into. In fact, I still make fun of them, but I was definitely whipped.

I had all the characteristics of a man who had fallen in love uncontrollably and viciously. That was definitely what happened.

I went through both physical and psychological transformation. I came home from school that year a little pudgy at 186 pounds. I never worked out at John Carroll. The Gold's Gym in Troy was three times as good as what they had at school. I was spoiled.

In about 30 days though I dropped 21 pounds. I was working out like a linebacker and looked ripped. My testosterone levels had probably doubled. I was jacked. Maja did not approve. She hectored me, "You know you're just going to die anyway right?"

"What are you talking about?"

"People like you think you can live forever by exercising but everyone dies eventually."

"Shut up. You're a Polack. I don't care about living forever."

"You're a Russian. That's far worse."

Maja ran me down a lot. My parents did as well so I was used to it. It must have felt normal to me. Perhaps her constant negativity brought us closer. That's disturbing but it may have been the truth. Now when I look back at it I am appalled at what I put up with. It was like having Leon Trotsky next to you all day long. Who the hell would want that?

I noticed a pattern here that has been pervasive throughout my life. I tend to let a lot of things go with a woman provided she is submissive in the bedroom.

As I will discuss in a later chapter, sexual dominance is the only kind of dominance that is an absolute deal breaker for me. When that occurs they simply have to go. Despite all the chronic complaining, Maja was sexually submissive. I drove all the action which is why I put up with the rest of it.

I was at the gym two hours a day which freaked her out. She wanted to know, "What was I white trash?" She used to harass me about lifting weights all the time. Maja said I was starting to look like an ape. Despite being a slave to love I knew she was lying. I looked great, almost as good as I did at 23 which was probably the year of my peak physical condition.

That summer women looked at me differently. It was noticeable. At age 19, I could put on muscle simply by looking at weights...and I was looking at a lot of iron.

What she feared was my pride. Maja did not want my business expanding into other markets. Maja had nothing to fear though. I could think of no one except for her. I was beyond obsessed. I thought our relationship was the greatest thing to ever happen to me.

We were both 19 and I was about to turn 20. Her body, despite all the smoking and zero exercise, was transcendent. Maja also no longer looked exotic in my mind. She was the standard for every woman.[11] Her gorgeous fake blonde hair fell to her shoulders and her eyes seemed bigger than tennis balls. Blue, large eyes with very dark skin, and a taut frame. There was a fine layer of muscle under her skin. The only fat she possessed was in the places where you'd pay to find it.

It was in the days when every girl wore Guess jeans. They fit the well-built woman perfectly, and Maja could have been a model for the product. One night we were in Cranbrook when the sun had just about faded. We were alone in a wooded area by the Greek outdoor theatre. She walked in front me and I could take the sight of those jeans no more. I reached out and pulled them down completely. I simply could not help myself.

I was demented by both love and lust. I hate to say it, but lust was definitely the junior partner. I was completely addicted to her in a manner I never was any drug. I began to call her "Buzzy" or "the Buzzy" due to her grooming habits in regards to a certain region of her body. I had never seen that before and it made quite an impression.

We went out every day until school started in late August.

Then things started getting weird. Maja made me promise not to tell people that we were going out. Then she also made me swear to tell no one that we were sleeping together. I kept only the second promise.

All of her friends were back in town at John Carroll. They were sophomores and were drinking it up. Suddenly she had people to do things with. I was no longer a priority.

At my current solitary age, I would welcome such a development, but back then I was all testosterone and dopamine. We fought quite often in the beginning of the school year. She wanted to keep it "casual." This was an impossibility as our relationship never was casual.

The berserker that was my love wanted nothing to change. If it did he would face his destruction in battle, high upon on a hill. No surrender, victory or death. That is how I saw it. I did not know it, but the battle would soon be upon me.

One great flaw with this story is that the Buzzy had been trying to break up with me ever since we first kissed. She did so half-heartedly, but it was always there. I did not know why at the time. She just kept yammering, "I don't want a boyfriend. I don't need this."

To which I would respond honestly: "Why not. This is great. I love you." I could have passed any lie detector you threw my way. I was completely sincere.

Maja would condescend that only I needed to "have someone." She did not. I was weak. She was strong, blah, blah, blah. Maja was real strong…provided you did not notice of any of her behaviors.

Now I know that all that psychobabble had nothing to do with me and everything to do with her father's (forced) abandonment of the family.[12] She was totally devastated by his departure and had difficulties dealing with men except at a superficial level.

At college, things got worse. Maja was trying to hit the eject button which made me highly unstable. Actually, that may be too kind of a description for what I was turning into. To quote Johnny Cash, "The beast in me is caged by frail and fragile bars."

I almost hit my roommate Jenkins for making her feel "uncomfortable" about the smell of sex after he entered the room one time after class. He lived there. He had a right to say whatever he wanted. I was way out of line. What Jenkins, the old fur ball, did not comprehend was that Maja was not a woman to me. She was a crusade.

My love had turned me into a psycho white knight. I am not a violent person. I never have been a violent person, but I would have chewed through the arms of any man who came between us. People noticed that I was radioactive. They started walking away from me. I was fine until her name was mentioned and then…yikes.

I had to be with her no matter what. We frequently slept together in each other's dorms. We even wore each other's t-shirts. She was not a typical woman as she bought extra larges. I kept one of those shirts for many years. It said, "John Carroll, the Ultimate Drinking Machine," underneath a BMW logo.

We went on a debate trip down to Otterbein in the middle of September. We were in a huge van. I was in the back seat next to Maja with our coats over us. It was chilly on the highway. Despite her lecturing me about my "sexual deviancy," in the middle of the trip, she decided it would be fun to jerk me off somewhere around Mansfield. A few of the guys heard some chaotic huffing and drew the proper conclusions. After that I was worshipped as a god by my fellow debaters.

As for the Buzzy, she never quite made it in debate. For one, she never understood it. You were supposed to…you know, debate. By this I mean that you had to respond to what your opponents said.

At that particular tournament, the old Miami assistant coach approached me in the hallway after he judged her novice round.

He tapped me on the shoulder. "Chapin, give me a Camel."

I handed him a Camel Light. In those days you could smoke in the hallways of college buildings. "Bern, tell me, that little one with the curves. The Spaniard. Is she your girlfriend?"

I was supposed to deny it, but his suddenness caught me off guard. "Yeah, how did you know?"

"Because she's running your anarchy brief and you don't share that stuff. Only, she has no idea what any of it means."

"I know, I know. I've told her what to say in rebuttals ten times. She refuses to listen to me. She says she'll figure it out but she still hasn't."

He laughed. "So she'll use your arguments but refuses to listen to you about how to defend them?"

"I'm afraid so."

"Love!" he said and began cracking up.

I nodded.

He continued. "She's really adorable man with that purple miniskirt and those gigantic blue eyes, but I don't think debate is in her future."

"Me neither." It wasn't. She quit after that semester.

One of my favorite memories of Maja though was when we were late for a tournament in October. She came bounding across the quad to the van. Maja did not know how to run and she bounced in a vertical rather than horizontal motion. She looked like a pogo stick. Her pigtails swirled over and under her head. I thought it was precious.

Yes, I was a total fool.

If you suspect that I had mixed feelings overall about the Buzzy you are correct.

Her disavowal of our relationship to others was completely ridiculous. Everyone knew we were "going out." I slept in her room and she slept in mine. Maja resented my limiting her options though.

How was she supposed to be a wild college girl with some 18th century character intruding upon her life all the time? I certainly was not "cool." I had no low profile in me. I loved her body and soul! I was all over her. I could not help myself. I was an all or nothing proposition. My devotion was slowly pushing her into the nothing camp. My high level of enthusiasm meant that I could be cut from the team soon.

Maja refused to call me her boyfriend. I felt disrespected. Her ~~friends~~ co-competing parasites sensed this and they hooked her up with some high-on in my class. He was about 5'10" and 125 pounds. A real trustafarian, yet that word had yet to be coined. He lived in my dorm on the floor below me. The tool was part of a frat that was about to have a Homecoming Dance. I do not remember what their Greek letters were but they wore green jackets. He duly asked her to go and she accepted.

This would have been perplexing to a rational male, but I interpreted it as a declaration of war. From age 21 to the present I would have simply accepted her treachery and been glad to distance myself from her.

Yet I was 20 and enamored with Maja. I did not approach the root of the problem. Instead, I tackled its symptom. I followed the guy in our dorm after dinner one day and got in his face. I screamed at him and waved my fists. Trustaman said nothing. He probably went back to his room and lit a bowl.

His brothers in the fraternity heard about this. They could not let my contempt for their insignia stand. I could not do that sort of thing to one of their boys.

Six of those pussies, without Captain Cannabis, came to my room to threaten me. Had it been eight months earlier I probably wouldn't have opened the door. I was more sensible then. Now I was looking for a resolution to this problem. I stoically accepted my fate and hoped to kill at least three of them in the resultant melee.

I flung open the door. "What?"

The lead one said, "Big tough guy huh? You stay away from our brothers or we'll kill you."

"You guys want to come in?" This request shocked them…a little. I was standing there out of my mind in a pair of boxer shorts with no shirt on. Blood was coming out of my ears. They did not accept my request.

They threatened me again, gave me the finger, and left. I never had any problems with those guys, although I certainly did worry about it for the next few months.

My friends were not going to help me. I was all alone. I was acting like such a musclehead they were tired of me. They were ready to feed me to the sharks themselves—and they would have been right to do so. I was a liability. I only cared about one person during that fall, and it was not me or any of them.

Yes, this tale really makes me look bad, really bad, but at least I learned from it. For the rest of my life, I never acted in this fashion again.

Maja was furious about what I did. She refused to talk to me for an entire night after the guy retracted his invitation to the dance. He cited her "lunatic Detroit friend" as being the reason. Besides he probably wanted to get back to the ganja.

Another bloke was interested in her. This time she would not tell me his name. He found out about me though and told her friend that he "could not compete. She had already found her man." What a fella!

Maja went ballistic over that statement. I was ruining everything for her. She said, "I shouldn't have even told you that. You're not even good looking. You look like someone who thinks he's something but isn't. You're nothing. Just a jerk with a haircut and Girbaud jeans."

Yet her actions suggested otherwise. It was not just me who was in love. It was frustrating for her, but far worse in Bernsville. Our romance had turned me into an angry and volatile young man. My appeal to women must have increased exponentially. One look at me and they could tell I was off my rocker.

I began working out at school again even though I never had previously. I had no choice. If I didn't start exercising I would have ate the walls.

Whenever I thought of the clown in the green frat jacket I doubled my poundage on the bench and the military press. I was getting stronger and also quite a bit crazier. I wanted revenge. I thought of putting the barbell through his head and through the skulls of the six guys at my door.

This was willful blindness on my part. We all know that it was not Trustaman upon whom I should have directed my venom. I was too much of a white knight to have been honest about it. The offending party was spared my rage entirely.

Maja and I continued our relationship thereafter. She lied to herself all day long about how she did not love me. Yet everything the Buzzy did disputed this. We kept sleeping together. We spent the next year-and-a-half arm-in-arm, but I never forgot about her faithlessness.

Honestly, I never forgave her. I never looked at her the same way after the dance incident. She was a traitor. My own jealousy and fury horrified me. You mean I was like that? Yes, I was.

I thought Maja had turned me into something horrid, but I had been that person all along. No matter. I never trusted her again. I cared less and less about her as each month passed by.

Our interest levels went in opposite directions. Maja soon gave up on letting me go. She started referring to me as her boyfriend. It was too late. The seeds of my rebellion had germinated.

By winter, Maja started to become possessive. At John Carroll she had a lot more clout than I did. That was not true on the road in the debate world. She stopped going to tournaments, but what was I doing in those hotels every other weekend?

The Buzzy knew the other debaters were harmless, but she wasn't so sure about me. I had told her about the events in Ann Arbor so what would stop me from rolling up on randoms at various colleges? Nothing as it turns out. She tried to keep my self-esteem as low as possible yet increasingly I was resistant to her "Bern is scum" message.

My friends at John Carroll were wild and she hated seeing me cavorting with them. She despised Sandy in particular who was dating many of the girls in her dormitory. Sandy was my best friend. Maja always wanted to know what we had in common. Quite a bit! With Sandy it was hard to say which one of us was the worse influence on the other.

My partner and I were one of the top teams in the Midwest and we had groupies. I turned them down for a while but that did not last. I was 20 after all.

The passionate love I had for Maja had largely dissipated by the time we got back to Detroit that summer. I went out constantly. I prospered. I had lots of opportunities I capitalized on.

I still loved the Buzzy but she was more friend than lover. By my senior year we were like brother and sister. I thought of her as a pal. She was an intellectual equal and I respected that…except for when it came to debate briefs. I enjoyed smoking and drinking coffee with her. That was about it. I would sleep over there and hold her only occasionally.

One night in March of 1991 she summoned me over to her dorm room. It was two months before I graduated. Maja was crying hysterically when I got there. She said that I had basically broken up with her by ignoring her. Thus, I was not her boyfriend anymore. I was happy to finally have my walking papers.

I laughed in her face. I got out of there quickly. There was something else in that room though. It was the phantom of that frat guy in the green jacket.

Unforgiven.

The next weekend I had a girl come up from Capital in Columbus. She stayed in my room. She was a debater who "wanted my advice."

In April, a month after Maja broke up with me officially, I picked up a girl who was 23 and who worked at a local restaurant. Somehow it got back to the Buzzy. She went to check her out and was astounded at my lust for such low company.

She stormed into my room. "I saw that girl. What does she have going for her except a hot butt? What?"

I broke into convulsions. Jenkins cracked-up too.

Maja immediately understood. "My God, I'm right. You sicko. You'd go out with a girl just because she had a hot butt? You're a degenerate!"

Welcome to the real world, Maja.

We continued to talk for a couple of years after that. Both serious girlfriends that followed her feared Maja's specter. They could tell she was bright and cultivated which was certainly not true of them. They hated Maja and forbid me from mentioning her name. I didn't. It was no loss. They did not understand that Maja had no more power over me than my friend Chris.

My parents were another story. They cherished Maja so much that I had to doctor the plot of our parting. I said she "dumped me." They were in mourning over it for a while. They wanted to blame me badly for the affair dissolving, but did not know enough about the facts to pull it off.

One day my father turned to me and said, "Maja was the love of your life." My dad had declared my life over at age 23.

He was wrong though. Maja was a scold and a grandmother to me; a constant critic. All of that I could have tolerated had she not driven me practically into a prison with the schemes she hatched in the fall of 1989.

Maja ran me down relentlessly for about a year until I finally gave her something to legitimately complain about. When I loved her she tried to escape. When my passion declined, hers heightened. It was not an unusual scenario for a man and woman.

Years later she gave me a book about St. Bernard of Clairvaux. That I was born on his death day to two atheist parents who knew nothing of the saint affected us both. I still have the book. She inscribed,

For your birthday—get yourself a great gift—
How about acquiring some virtue.

Same old Maja!

Had I known more about psychology at the time, I would have realized that she may have been my father's greatest love…which is not a road I feel like traveling down too far. Only now, at my advanced age, do I fully comprehend that no man has politically correct fantasies about women. It could be that he was massively envious of me and longed to be in my shoes. Oh well, let's drop it. Allow dad to rest in peace.

I saw her occasionally when I returned to Detroit in the nineties. She had married a guy from John Carroll. He was also from Detroit and I knew him. We once went to a Tigers game together. A fine fellow. He was definitely a safe choice. I am sure he is a good provider.

The last time I saw her was in 1997. We met at a coffee shop. She was still smoking. I had quit. I had not seen her in two years. I knew no Manosphere lingo back then, but she had definitely hit the wall.

Dental school had taken a toll on her. She was never heavy or even puffy, but the Buzzy had lost a good 10 pounds. The layer of muscle that so shaped her legs, arms, and butt was gone. Maja looked strung out. Her jeans hung shapelessly. Her flawless thighs were but a memory. Her face was drawn and her big eyes were tired. All she talked about was studying.

I never called her again but there was one final incident. I came across one of her friends from John Carroll at the St. Michael's Street Fair in 2001. She seemed to be digging me so I reached over and kissed her on the lips for a few minutes.

This quickly got back to the Buzzy. At about 11:20 pm I heard my phone ring and hang up quickly. No message was left. The caller ID said "PRIVATE." The phone rang again. I watched it. Again there was no message.

I had missed a major lecture by not picking up which pleased me greatly.

Thus ended the reign of Maja the Buzzy, daughter of Ecthelion.

On that funeral pyre went memories of a Bern I never wanted, along with rage and obsession I have not displayed since. I was young and naïve. I am very glad those days are over, although to have those levels of testosterone just one more time…

Chapter 4: The MGTOW Moment

When the going gets weird, the weird turn pro.
          —Hunter S. Thompson

There are no good girls gone wrong—just bad girls found out.
          —Mae West

MGTOW was an acquired taste. It slowly arose as a result of my personal history and was augmented by information acquired in my thirties. I had lucky beginnings as we saw in the last chapter. Up until age 33 or so, I was giddily addicted to women. There was little carnage. There was pain with pleasure, but I understood the occupation in which I was employed. Bad news came with the territory. No arrests, false accusations, surprise abortions or DNA tests came my way.

I had so many positive experiences until that time with the opposite sex that there was no reason for my outlook to change. With women, I worshipped the Plus-minus Statistic. According to the way it was kept, I was heading for a 12 year career in the NHL and maybe a plaque bearing my name and retired number on the side of the stadium.

Let me explain. It's a hockey statistic I applied to a man's sleeping partners. In the NHL, a player's plus-minus rating means very little in regards to his talent two weeks into the season, but, by the end of the year, in my opinion, it tells the whole story.

The number represents the goal differential that transpires during the time when you are on the ice. You get a +1 for every goal in which you are present and a -1 when the other team scores on you. The career plus-minus leaders are all in the NHL Hall of Fame, and one of our DRW[13] guys, Nicholas Lidstrom, holds the number 10 position on that list.

My childhood memories are never far away so one day, back in the late nineties, I reflected on Paul Ysebaert's rating of +44 for the 1991-1992 season. It was a big deal in Detroit. Soon after, I thought about women. They were always at the apex of my attention span in those days. I then applied the statistic to how many girls one slept with. The + represented the score and the – was your age.

I have no idea where my stats were on that day but my numbers soon blossomed. At the time of my divorce, when I was 25, I was -20 and headed for the minors in Thunder Bay, yet I recovered quickly and only slowed down at around age 38 or so.

If we count this year as the end of my career I would still be at a respectable number. I could have done better but it stopped mattering to me in 2003. I was only too happy to "say goodbye to all that."

It was in the summer of 2002 that I started to realize that what I thought I wanted was actually an illusion.

My present attitude can be traced back to a certain moment 14 years ago. That's when it started, when I began to imagine that life without women was possible. I know the exact month. After that, I never stopped questioning the female-centric life I had constructed for myself.

There were glimmerings of its coming earlier. Once, in college, I walked into a party and saw two couples holding each other and singing Bob Marley's "No Woman No Cry." They had changed the lyric to "No Woman No Pride." It was beastly. I stopped, looked at them, and thought the guys lobotomized. Then I moved on. Sadly, I drew no greater conclusions from the incident.

July and August of 2002 was the oddest of times. I had reached the pinnacle of my powers in terms of "game." Oh, I was never a pickup artist, not even close. Indeed, due to my interests completely conflicting with those of women, I was always irritated by having to be in their presence for an extended duration.

I was not "a woman's man" in terms of achievement, and I also had zero desire to be a woman's man at any level.

I was aware of Mystery and some of the other PUAs. I did not doubt their effectiveness, and I still respect their knowledge of feminine psychology. Yet magic tricks and flamboyant clothes were too great a sacrifice for sex in my mind. I don't like having fingernails and I despise jewelry. I own two watches and they never leave my shelf.

My idea of peacocking was going to work, buying and selling real estate, and going to the gym on a daily basis. How many women think well of these habits is unknown. The only important thing is that they were MY habits.

As men age our testosterone levels decline, but, at 32, I was still full of juice. Unlike today, most of the women who "dug me" in 2002 were legitimately attractive. I wanted to fool around with them to one degree or another. It was always their personalities that turned me off, but I generally liked what I saw (and imagined seeing).

That was before the days of widespread online dating. It was back when you needed courage to get up there and swing a bat at the plate. The bravest men would approach groups of six or eight females and start talking. I was not one of those men.

Pick-up artists would ridicule my *best move* which was to hold my hand out to passing females and say, "Hi, I'm Bernard." Pretty stupid. There are all sorts of reasons why such a tactic would not be effective but it opened the door to the usual utterances one would expect from a guy who kissed the Blarney Stone.

I would also yell "where are you going? I'm right here" as they came by. I might tap them on the shoulder and ask, "What are we doing later?" This often resulted in some opportunities. The best one I can recall occurred when Frankie and I stood next to two six foot tall beauties at Melvin B's on the Gold Coast. It turned out that they were beach volleyball players.

I walked up to the girls and said, "Ladies, where are we going after this?" They proceeded to smile. They were genuinely receptive. This frightened us both! It was entirely unanticipated. I only did it because they were scary and out of our league. I wanted to look like a hero to my friend. I hoped he would tell others about my Spartan *sang-froid*.

Frankie shirked his duty immediately. He was thoroughly intimidated. He turned around and would not even look in their direction. Now I had no wingman. It did not matter. I was going to fuck up the interaction with or without him. I gave off only simian efforts at conversation thereafter.

Most of the confidence I displayed to females was fraudulent. I have always been confident about my intellect, creativity, and general abilities. Spearman's G as it were. Yet I never confused my actual merits with anything women would appreciate. Cognitive capacity in men is not prized by the opposite sex. My old friend Dr. G once rebuked me about this back in Royal Oak. He said, "Stop doing that stuff."

"What?"

"Talking to women about books, history, literature, art, etc. Don't let them know you're smart. That's not going to help you. It's a mistake. They don't want any of that."

I thought he was wrong. Later, I realized Dr. G was right.

The worst was telling them about my profession. Over the years, scores of women looked appalled after I told them I was a psychologist. They were more than put off. Could I read their minds they wanted to know? Would I "psycho-analyze" them?

How could I do that? I am not a psychoanalyst. Never mind the fact that most psychoanalysts are scammers anyway in my opinion. I honestly thought they had confused "psychologist" with witch doctor based on their reactions.

Moreover, most school psychologists only work with children. Adults are outside of their daily experience. They are also uniformly female[14] and progressive in orientation which means they know practically nothing about anything. I was an exception, of course, but most school psychologists can only think within the lollypop framework of human nature.

I still recall the shock on one of their faces during a meeting after a caseworker said she did not tell the female students in her care that she was pregnant.

My deluded peer asked, "Why not?"

I answered for the caseworker. "Because the girls will try to hurt her either out of jealousy or to take advantage of her."

The female school psychologist looked at me as if I was Satan. "Noooo" she chided. "Why not? Tell me." As if asking another woman directly while pretending I was not present would yield an answer that pleased her.

The caseworker declined to lie. "No. He's right. They would try to punch me in the stomach." My peer was crestfallen. She said nothing to me after that and gave me the cold shoulder for several days. I am sure she then purged the memory from her cranium and went back to thinking that all of us lived on the set of the 1970s theatrical *Hair*.

A few women though, upon hearing of my profession, reflexively asked me if I thought they were crazy. This was just a few moments after we were met! I would say, "How would I know mam? But that those were the first words out of your mouth is so…well, it's…rather incriminating isn't it?"

They knew they were nuts and they did not want anyone else to know about it. They tried to hide from my male gaze thereafter. One can only imagine the nature of their felonious careers; rough riding over the carcasses of everyone unfortunate enough to encounter them. Lying incessantly and taking responsibility for nothing. Turning the tables habitually and accusing others of their crimes. Projections tossed hither thither as if they were trying out at the NFL combine. They had to be avid practitioners of the Chapin Theory of Female Crypsis in its most embryonic state. Despite their privilege, I was glad their life was not mine.

We used to call meeting women "work" which is exactly what it was. Hard labor filled with beatings, housings, disrespect, and soul searching. In college we made fun of guys who got rejected. That gynocentric garbage luckily ended with graduation. As adults all of us clapped for the hardest working members of the crew.

Many of my best approaches were done more out of a desire to impress Duke and Bill than to obtain someone's phone number. Valorous behavior was highly prized. I would see several attractive women in a corner and then sprint off initiating one ruse or another. The decisions were sudden. Had I thought about it I would have realized I was walking into Corregidor.

There was great camaraderie in those days. They used to call me "Fire" because as Duke said, "Your hair man. *It's on Fire!*" We would all sing "Gotta have gotta have work! Let's fill the order!" It was all quite silly but I think the manufactured high spirits were necessary. You could not be depressed and do what we did.

My favorite memory from that period was when a woman turned and said as we entered a Christmas party, "Oh look, the mafia is here."

In general, I confined my efforts to groups of women no larger than four. If there was some indication of interest I would approach. If there was no outright indication, I might still rush in if they were relatively sedate and not talking at one another with the intensity of Al Pacino.

I once said to my friend after we saw two women at a bar gibbering to each other like fanatics. "Dog. You know what they're talking about? Fucking nothing, nothing man." He found this humorous and I have no doubt that my assessment was accurate.

I was never reliable though. You could not count on me with women. I "worked" in calculated bursts of activity. If they were receptive I was always there to help, but most women were not receptive. Sometimes I would pussyfoot around and expect others to do my work for me.

I still remember being out with Duke and Bill one night when they had been flying around like wasps yet I was acting like a voyeur. Duke slapped my shoulder, "Fire" he said. "I think it's time for you to go out there and Fire it up. Isn't it time though?"

Bill jumped in. "Yeah though. Fire? Fire afraid to go out there and take a beating? Not like you, Fire. Fire it up!"

Generally, I listened. I cared a lot more about their opinions than I did those of the women we met. I was no player but my output was far beyond anything my father ever dreamed of. The world had changed as a result of the sixties counter-culture becoming *the* culture. We profited from that change on many a night even if the overall result will sink both my country and western civilization.

Even as a young man though I disliked one night stands. I did not feel comfortable having people I did not know in my apartment. The optimal outcome for me was physical relations starting on the second date. It rarely worked out that way. I always paid for the girl so my courtship was time limited. I probably would have liked it if the girls paid half but I grew up in another era. I have heard from the younger guys that many women insist on paying their way so that they do not owe the man anything. Unfortunately, I never met any women like that.

What I looked for on a first date was not contact, but, rather, a sense that she liked me or was interested. Often their indifference, real or premeditated, meant that I never called them again. I had no desire to be their "friend" or beta boy.

All told, if you look at my history in the context of a baseball batting average, before July-August of 2002, my finest performance was to bat no better than .350 with the women I asked out. Most times, the majority of the ones I approached blew me off or were completely non-responsive. They "weren't interested." They "had boyfriends." They were "too busy."

Who cared what the reasons were? I stopped being vested once their faces darkened. I knew what the answer would be. It was all very irrational. I recall a time in 2001 when I called a girl who gave me her number. Instead of being nice to me she issued a lecture on the "aggressive behavior" I exhibited on the night we met. She had no complaints at the time! I flipped off the phone and hung up on her. This presaged my current mentality.

Dates were a regular occurrence. I went out with women constantly between 1991 and 2008. It was an integral part of each week. Regardless of the negative experiences I had, I always marched right back in there to receive more punishment. It felt right. It was what I was *supposed* to do. I thought blowing all my money on women and nights out was what men did.

I knew though that other things were more essential to my identity such as reading, writing, and working out, but none of those activities gave me the high that sexual encounters did. I was constantly chasing the dragon.

Disagree I would if someone had said that I was completely preoccupied with finding women. Yet my response would have been a lie. Nothing else compared to the energy I put forth in trying to obtain them.

My drive was not strictly sexual. It pains me to say it now, but I wanted to find a wife. I wanted to be a father. It was not just society that made me want to do those things. I deeply felt it.

We used to hit all the big street fairs in Chicago. The summer of 2002 started out no differently than any other. Everyone would drink heavily and you could just walk around greeting various groups of women. We did the same thing that year that we did the year before. The results were not the same, however.

Somewhere around the middle of 2002 I sharply departed from all historical benchmarks. At the Sheffield Street Fair, I witnessed the first evidence that the stars had become realigned. I asked three women out that night…but they all said yes. I did not think too much of this. It was a good showing. I called them back that week. To my surprise, the numbers worked and the girls were welcoming. Curious.

I arranged various times to rendezvous and they all were present and on time. They were interested. I cannot recall how intimate these encounters became but they at least were positive. No drama.

The way it works in the schools is that you get your remaining paychecks for the year at the end of June. This has to last you until August so you need to budget. Ordinarily this was no problem for me, but none of the girls wanted to meet just for coffee. My bank balance was endangered. No matter, I trudged forward. I had to do it. It was a question of duty!

The next weekend I asked out three more girls at a different street fair. Affirmative answers all around. I was now batting 6 for 6 in a week's time. Very odd. That never happened even with a small sample size. I managed to not call two of the girls from the week before, but I had already set up a meeting for the third. I was running out of days for the coming week. When I was younger I would have felt like a swordsman, but at 32 I was already calculating my risk of ruin.

Bill and Duke noticed that I was not getting rejected. They talked about me being on a serious heater. They thought me a lucky talisman.

The next weekend I was more brazen. I wanted to get rejected. I had no more money or time for this hogwash. I marched into situations that most men would have avoided. I ignored obvious signs of hostility and kept talking anyway. Yet those girls proved receptive too. I was becoming a role model.

Bill and Duke did not know what to make of it. I was a machine. I was a bricklayer. To quote Cake, "if you want to have cities you've got to build roads." I was building roads, and laying the groundwork for everyone else. That weekend I went 4 for 4 bringing my streak to 10 out of 10. All of the girls were younger than me and met my standards for sexual attraction which were galaxies higher than they are today.

What the hell happened? I had become the stud I always wanted to be. Was this the happy time that u-boat captains used to speak of? Not really. I had a profound sense of unease. Out of the catch, I knew all of their faces but was not sure which face to mentally match with a name.

At home I stared at my answering machine warily. Often it was lit up with four or five messages at a time. I have never enjoyed the wooing aspect of dating, but talking to all of those women proved an excruciating endeavor. They had little to say and I was unsuccessful at getting them off the phone.

One of them noticed my impatience, observing, "So you're just calling to get a time to meet up? You don't want to talk to me, right? Seems like you have to run or something." That was correct. I definitely did not wish to "conversate" with her. I was not even sure I wanted to fool around with her at that point. No matter. My indifference was intoxicating. She could not get enough of me and "couldn't wait" for our date.

Generally, the more women I romanced the less respect I had for them as a group. What kind of person is attracted to somebody who wants little to do with them? Not me, but it seemed true for the ornate sex.

Much is made of that Groucho Marx line that he wouldn't want to be part of a club that would have him as a member. Yet that has never meshed with my psychology. Billions of humans on this earth don't know my name and don't care about me. I accept this, but I do not want to waste any time or money on them. When girls who liked me played hard to get or appeared flighty, I quickly disappeared. I wanted to yell at them, "I'm not like you! I'm a mature adult."

I kept going out with the girls and was bleeding cash like a rapper with a thirty man entourage. My two credit cards were toast. I could pay only the minimum on them that month. I was no longer sure that I would have enough money to pay for the gas I needed to drive my car to work in a few weeks.

I thought about going to a loan shark. Instead, I turned to Bill, the richest guy I knew.

I walked over to his stately pad that he shared with Duke in the New York building.

Bill was watching a soap opera instead of trying to sell his software. The foolish company he worked for guaranteed him $80,000 a year plus commission. They did not realize that Bill—the master salesman—thought 80k was just fine. He needed no commission to do everything he wanted so he did not bother with working at all. He coasted all year before jumping ship for another company. The man had incredible skills. Every start up sought his services.

He greeted me at the door in boxers and a t-shirt. "Fire, what the hell do you want? It's 10 am."

"Bill, I need a favor."

"What?"

"I cannot afford to go out with all of these women, but I have to ride this streak out man. It's destiny. I've never been this hot in my life."

"None of us were ever as hot as you are now. So what? What is this the National Bank of Swieca?"

"Listen man, I'm not going to be able to keep it up without a cash infusion of some kind. I'll have to go belly up and quit."

"Fire, stop taking these girls to the Raw Bar. They're not worth it. Take them to the IHOP."

"You know I can't take them to the IHOP."

"Stop being so stupid. Just meet them at bars for a drink."

"Done! But they order 9 dollar glasses of wine at the bar. Many of them make me look like a teetotaler. They're heavy drinkers man. It's gruesome."

"Fire, those are the easiest kind to have sex with. Pull yourself together. You're attitude…it sucks man it really does. You sound like a loser."

"Look, Bill, I need a loan…seriously. This whole caper is going to fall apart without more dinero."

"What? Like 20 bucks?"

"Come on, Bill. Don't make me beg. At least 200. I'll pay you back."

"Yeah, you'll pay me back with like quarters every week."

"Well, how about if I agree to 220 for 200. That way you get some interest. Give me a month." This really was a better option than a loan shark as 1. Bill wouldn't break my legs and 2. I wouldn't have to pay a 10% weekly vigorish.

Bill sat down. He thought about it for a while. "No Fire. No interest. You'll pay me back exactly what you owe, but I have one stipulation."

"What's that?"

"You join JDate with me. I expect your profile up on there by the end of the day."

"What? I can't afford a dating website. I also don't have time to finagle anyone else."

"No problem. It is one week free of charge. They're running a special. Email me your dating profile so I can laugh at your antics on there. That's the interest charge. Boy those girls are going to turn you into chum. They'll eat you alive. You're soft."

"You mother fucker."

"Oh, the fun we'll have."

"We're not even Jewish."

"So, your name's Bernard. Sell it baby! Sell it! Use your skills."

He laid out 10 twenties and I took the money.

For the next month, Bill called me "CobaltBlue" as that was the name I had for the week on JDate. I quickly got four meet-ups for the site thus raising my batting average to 14 for 14.

I proved a poor salesman. All of the girls accused me of being a Fugazi. They knew I was not Jewish. Yet, for some reason, none of them suspected Bill.

I physically looked the part. I had brown eyes and brown hair. I had a graduate degree. I was a psychologist. What the hell! My name was practically Bernie.

Meanwhile Bill, with his blue eyes, blond hair, and Polish last name, met their smell test…which was ridiculous. Walk like a duck, talk like a duck, and not be a duck. They thought it added up though. Bill was Kosher in their eyes while the guy with legitimately Russian grandparents was bacon. What a bunch of fruitcakes!

That marked the end of my streak: 14 for 14. Now I had to deal with the consequences. Quickly, a few of them fell off the Bern-wagon, and I was dispirited by spending nearly all of my weekday nights in noodle shops. I was subjected to the most asinine of conversations. Large swaths of my life was wasted on interrogations and absorbing trivial monologues.

I still recall one of the girls harassing me about why I did not have my own private practice. Why wasn't I ambitious? Why did I want to be a grunt making only 44 grand for the rest of my life?

I stared at her with detestation. I asked her if she had parents. Then I asked if those parents ever explained to her why it was rude to ask so many personal questions. Apparently they had not. I could not wait to get out of there.

Several of the girls I walked home to their apartments on those first dates. Stuff did happen inside. It did not matter to me by that point. I was not pleased feeling obligated to them. Sex or even second base meant that I had to keep calling them and hearing nonsensical warbling in my ear for yet another week.

By the time work started up in August I had abandoned the whole project. I stopped calling any of the 14. I felt like I was lucky to still be sane. I had new status among my male friends though. Several associates inquired about me hanging out with them so they could witness "my magic" and profit from it.

I was done though. I simply wanted my old life back and having a bank account with more than two digits in it. I longed for retirement.

As the month of August wore on and my birthday passed, I realized that what I thought I wanted out of life was not what I really wanted. I was no longer sure about "dating." I did not get along with those people. I did not like them. I did not want to be around inquisitors.

I stopped reading my pickup artist stuff. I put the books back in the closet. I did not want game. Most of all I did not want to have to ingest the story of a new girl's life each week.

In the future, I was more taciturn when I met a girl. I could tolerate the cross-examinations less and less. I was not animated. I lacked zeal. I knew the story was going to end badly one way or another. I also refused to talk about myself. I told them I was not interesting and that we should talk about something else. They accommodated me by being only too happy to drone on about the shallowissitudes of their souls. I sort of listened yet I knew a Rubicon had been crossed.

I was no longer the man I used to be. I had left those shores.

It was at that moment—through dating 14 women simultaneously—in the summer of 2002 that I knew I was done with the business. I no longer wanted to be an interviewee. The 14 had forced a red pill down my throat. It dissolved and then dispersed throughout my body, dying me scarlet. The ink proved permanent. What I thought I wanted was not what I wanted.

A year later, I became a men's rights activist and wrote weekly pieces for *Men's News Daily*. A heretic had been born. A rebel I remain.

Chapter 5: Sex is a False God

There are two types of heterosexual men in this world. One fantasizes about women in their twenties and the other lies and says they do not.

Joke: *A man goes to a prostitute. He takes his clothes off and she begins laughing at the size of his member. She says, "Who are you going to satisfy with that?" "Myself!" he answers.*

Like trips to the barber, my time at bars and clubs is no more.

I do not miss it. I am happy to be retired. Yet it is conventional wisdom that most men live and die for sex. Not me. Not anymore.

Even when I felt certain of eventually obtaining coitus, I often could not tolerate all the dates and the process necessary to secure it. I am not a mangina. I have no female interests or topics of commonality with the opposite sex. Getting along with them is a serious challenge.

While our society worships sex, I regard it as being a false god. I remain passionate about women's bodies, but my ardor no longer blinds me to the realities of actually having to deal with them.

Yes, sex still motivates…a little. This is more due to the testosterone buzz I experience upon seeing an attractive woman than anything else. I love looking at them. They make me feel wired and they stimulate dopamine release. My eyes are in it for the hormones, but it would be false to say that I am attached to them for any other reason.

I love male-gazing upon scantily clad women at the gym, the beach or in breastaurants like Hooters. Ask these women out though, that I do not do. I have zero interest in talking to them. What would we talk about? What would I have to offer them? To ask these questions is to answer them.

It really does not matter. Unlike Adam Ant, I am not serious and I am not desperate. Being sexually "desperate" or "thirsty" (as they say in our vapid vernacular) does not describe me.

If I permitted myself to look at pornography or tumblr photos on a daily basis I would certainly feel frustrated, but I choose not to do those things. What's the point? I realize now that those delectable women will never be a part of my life again. I accept that. There is no reason to delude myself. I refuse to go mad being obsessed with what I cannot possibly obtain.

On my Youtube channel, we often talk about the personality differences when it comes to politics between the left and the right. The leftists are obsessed with what others have. They are jealous and wrathful towards "the rich" or the "one percent" or whatever group they can pour their bile upon.

I am not a leftist. I refuse to process life through a covetous lens. I do not envy another man's woman or his trappings. If he is doing better than me I take my hat off to him. While I would love to have an indoor hot tub it is not an economic possibility for me. So what? Does that mean I am the victim of a conspiracy?

The same can be said in regards to spending sensuous hours with a 25-year-old hard body. It won't happen. This realization does not make my days melancholic. Hard bodies are not in my future so let's focus on something else instead. Those men who refuse to accept these eventualities are the men who become despondent with age. I know a guy like that. He inspired me to pen:

Few non-drug addicted people are more cringe
inducing than the aging extrovert.

The fellow misses the constant companionship of having women in his orbit. Without it, he will sit and talk to anyone…including me. I will be walking on the treadmill with a book open and he will gibber at me for an hour straight.

I am very glad to be an introvert, and I have no longing for that past youthful environment in which your associates blather all day long.

Indeed, I admit that my case may be unusual, but the only time I have had feelings of loneliness was when I was among people I did not like. In that context I felt trapped. When alone though…I feel free.

I eschew depression. I will not fixate on what is gone. The past is the past. I will focus on tomorrow. It is better to be grateful to God for what you already possess and what you will experience in the future.

When I was a young man I occasionally had romantic dreams. By this I mean dreams in which I had serious feelings for a woman. Generally, the plot involved a girl and I being in love in some strange setting. We did all sorts of touristy or brave things. I would then awake in a devastated state. I felt loss.

Needless to say, it's been over 15 years since I have had any of those dreams. My unconscious knows better. I understand myself and also understand the opposite sex. For me now, romance is largely delusion. There will be no more of that.

Romance I do not miss. I have an imagination that satiates my physical longings. I have no use for prostitution. I have no moral objection to it, but I do not wish to contract such services for myself. I fear both the disease aspect of "paying for it" and also the illegality intrinsic to that arrangement. It's simply not for me but I respect your diversity when it comes to your own choices.

In the last chapter we saw that my past perceptions of desire were not matched by my actual desires. I faded away after I got what *I thought* I wanted.

A famous evolutionary psychologist wrote that "within every man beats the heart of a harem master."[15] That was probably still true of me at age 32, but my mind realized that I could not accept the hurdles I needed to jump in order to reach that goal.

Now, at 46, the type of woman I can obtain does not match my fantasies in the least. She is not a "goal." She's more of a consolation prize; a prize that will merely heighten the levels of agitation I sometimes experience.

In my opinion, the "love response" is something that cannot be triggered by a woman in her forties or over. A woman's youth and beauty are key factors behind a man's ability to fall in love with her. Biological anthropologist Dr. Helen Fisher wrote an excellent work called *The Anatomy of Love* which educates greatly on this subject.

Men fall in love when they are younger, and, most importantly, when the woman is younger. When you are dealing with females who are at their estrogenic peak (age 20 or so) your autonomy is constantly threatened. You begin to lose control over your feelings. You become obsessed. The only reason that it does not happen with older men is because we are not exposed to younger women. It's easy to talk tough with a 45-year-old beater and I frequently do.

I fell in love ten or twelve times before age 35 but now it's a non-issue. Most of the women I meet are my age and it is very unlikely I could develop feelings towards them. Its occurrence is almost unseemly to contemplate.

My sexual attraction towards women is usually blunted by several factors including their age, obesity, disinterest in physical activity/movement, dominating natures, triviality, incessant monologues concerning their children or petty daily events, and their complete ignorance of history, politics, and psychology (except for what they hear from Dr. Oz). How can you fall in love with someone whose mind, regardless of job title, suggests that they are nothing more than an oxidizing clerk?

These are the facts. All that emotive stuff was in the past. There is no point in lamenting its passing. What's done is done. The disparity between my desires and my backbencher reality is another reason why I am a Man Going His Own Way. I don't want what they're selling.

In the way of example, let me compare women to shoes. Dating as an older man is akin to walking into a store and picking out a pair of shoes. You like them. You give them to the clerk and ask that he gets you a pair in your size (mine are 10.5). He replies, "Certainly, we have those in size 7. I'll go get them now."

When you protest to the fellow that you wear a size 10.5 he ignores your statement and disappears into the backroom. When he reappears he hands you the 7s. Voila! What a store. Any color you want as long as it's black![16] That is me at the moment. I am presented with a series of unappealing choices so it is better not to buy at all.

That was a somewhat absurd example. However, dating the modern older woman is equally absurd. You are the customer and they are the store. You are advised to wedge your foot into whatever shoe they give you.

No thanks.

You can't make a dog a cat, and you cannot morph an obese flibbertigibbet into an object of desire. I want what I want and if I cannot get it—or something in the neighborhood of it—I will buy nothing. Happily I will come home empty handed.

This brings me to obesity which could be an independent chapter given its insidious effects upon male sexual desire. My friend Bill used to joke all the time about us "bringing home bigguns!"

On my Youtube channel, we make great hay out of "BTB."

BTB is when I report my weight and then jokingly tell my subscribers to obtain a *Bigger Than Bern* female. As I type this I am 222 pounds and have had no end of difficulty, as of late, in finding a woman who is well below my own weight. It really should not be that challenging!

I once had a female co-worker ask me about this. She fed me the typical propaganda: "Well, if you really liked them then it wouldn't matter."

I laughed. "Of course it would matter. If they don't look female then how the hell am I going to *really like* them?" You cannot get a glimpse of what you covet if it is slathered with lipidized takeout breakfasts and lunch time feasts.

The fools actually think they can shame and manipulate males into altering their sexuality.

The career of Melissa McCarthy suggests that future action films may well feature BTB actresses that nobody wants to look at. Hollywood is dedicated to reprogramming male sexuality one biggun at a time. Good luck to them! I advise young men to boycott her films, and not to support a misandric entertainment industry in general. Cutting off my cable was the smartest thing I ever did.

As disgusting as McCarthy's physique is, she is not too far off from the American norm. No, I am not cut and pasting Wal-Martian photos in for my analysis. It's a fact. The weight of American women is increasing by blimps and mounds.

Time Magazine just ran an article claiming that 40 percent of American women are obese. That word is not synonymous with "overweight" which meets a…ah, lighter definition. By that definition, 60 percent of American women are larger than the pale.[17]

It is worse for women than men: "Now, a new study reveals that while obesity rates in men have plateaued, rates have continued to rise among women."[18]

"Obesity" is not just a few pounds over. It's Velveeta. You cannot tell where the stomach ends and the hips begin. In short, it's absolutely revolting.

If the hourglass shape is ideal—and it certainly is for me—then what do bovine characteristics do to male desire? They kill it. We love curves. We do not love spheres.

Yes, what goes by the description of "curvy" in 2016 is all too often a "sphere." I say no waist is a total waste. How are we supposed to pretend that this cellulite epidemic is not an issue? A round mound of buffet down is not what most men fantasize about in a sexual partner.

Unfortunately, for the last two years, I have been on the front lines of the porcine-palooza. All of the women I met were single mothers which is to be expected in the suburbs. The conversations were barbarous. Their endless talking about their children still baffles me. Why did they constantly gibber about another man's offspring with me? I mentioned this behavior to a friend of mine who is my age. He nodded his head and said, "That's all they have. They have nothing else on their minds."

On the positive side, I noticed that the Indiana ladies were less neurotic and irritable than most of the women my age in Chicago. They were less angry as well.

What did not gratify me was that their personalities did not matter due to obesity. Their builds were not even remotely attractive. Oh, the pictures they sent were fine but what I met was a different creature. The images they uploaded on the dating site were not representative of what they actually looked like.

One of the first girls I met out had snapshots of herself in her twenties when she was in fact 40. I did not realize that because she was a different ethnicity and I thought, "they don't wrinkle like we do." Well, her face was not wrinkled, but her body was overlaid with rice chex.

When I arrived at the restaurant to meet her she approached me and tapped me on the shoulder. I had no idea who she was. The woman was 50 pounds heavier than her photos. What on earth was she doing? How could a person be so deluded? It was the epitome of false advertising. I sat there stunned; after forty-five minutes, I high-tailed it home. I guess she buys into the lie that "if men like me it won't matter what I look like." Of course we care what you look like. We're men.

This scene repeated itself several times. Eventually, I closed my account. What was the point? I am not a pig farmer.

The women I met were 30 pounds (at least) heavier than their pictures. Twenty pounds over I can accept. Thirty pounds over acts like reverse Viagra. The fib represented in their dating profiles nauseated me.

Why would they do that? Somewhere down the line they must have learned that deceit pays off. What they did would be akin to me taking photos of myself in a baseball cap to hide the fact that I was bald. Even worse, it would be like me posting pictures from my early 30s back when I still had hair. I would never do that. It's dishonorable, and I would hate to see the look of contempt flashed upon meeting me. I have shame. They do not.

The facts are that despite what all of us know to be true, many women continue to believe that men have only a passing interest in their bodies. This is ludicrous. What exactly do these duplicitous women online think that men are going to like them for? An innate need for criticism and redirection? I have no such needs. Neither do you. With the opposite sex, their personalities are the tax and their bodies are the dividend.

Indeed,

A woman's physique is the eternal dividend you receive
for investing in an extremely disorderly company.

Without the legs, without the derriere, without the breasts, without the stomach you are left with an organization whose books are in complete disarray. Without the chassis, no man would finance an entity facing liquidation and unruly creditors. An obese woman is akin to a firm whose CEO just got jailed. That stock is going to zero. Keep pretending it's not a problem and you may well become the next Enron.

When the curves are gone there is no reason for a man to stay. Do you want to be condemned to living in close proximity with a woman whom you dread seeing naked? I don't. If it's a choice between that and isolation I will take Devil's Island any time.

In my opinion, sex is either good or bad depending on the woman's build. If her form is excellent then the sex is excellent. I am a simple man. I do not need them to do much of anything. If the shape is right it is a fine night! Conversely, if her body is terrible then I will never know what the sex is like because I would fly back to my exurban enclave beforehand.

I grant that many would say I am missing something with my sexual evaluation. Yes, there are many other variables, but I am the sort of fellow who can entertain himself. A healthy infrastructure equals big fun.

I once had a friend try to justify why he did not mind that his wife had turned into a cottage cheese dowager. He said, "A warm hole is a warm hole."

I stared at him as if he were insane. "Jack" I said. "Now you're lying to both of us. You know that is not true. What would stop you from having sex with men or even ostriches if that were the case? Why are you trying to deceive both of us?"

He made no comment. Jack knew that what he said was preposterous, but he hoped to convince himself otherwise.

Additionally, I have noticed that over the years all of the women I went out with made some sort of comment about how "they did not want to lose me as a friend." They considered me to be an exquisite conversational companion. The feeling did not run both ways. I was not their friend. My feelings for them were as conditional as their feelings were for me.

How can you be friends with someone who confuses criticism with hate? A "friend" is a person with whom you can speak to frankly. That has not been the reality with most of the women I knew. I always had to address them carefully and with a mental editor on hand. You are not allowed to redirect a woman in any way yet they expect to help run your life.

Who wants to be around a bunch of people with whom you have to walk on conversational glass? That is not a friendship. That's an ordeal. You cannot be amigos with a person you have to treat "special."

If any women read this book (and that is not advised) you should listen to your Uncle Bern. The idea that men will like you regardless of what you look like is an incredible error. If men fell in love based on personality they would have dated their best friends starting in high school. Female anatomy is what enthralls us and when that frame loses its vibrancy the woman loses her authority. Straight talk!

That is why there are so many women who will not retire from their jobs. If they could not be supervisors then they would have to deal with others as equals. They have Deposed Queen Syndrome. They do not want to interact with proles on the street. They are better than the rest of us. Says who? Their job title. Without that they would have no power whatsoever. No bestowed authority and they are just another pylon at the mall. Being in a position of power is the only way older women can get any attention. That's why they never want to retire completely.

Young lady, take my opinions as the gospel. That will save you an incredible amount of time and expense. Get a gym membership. Don't listen to your female friends. Forget about your nails and tan, skip dessert instead. Shun a media that intentionally lies to you (more clicks!) along with television shows that merchant female misperception and then morph it into glossy dramas and mindless situation comedies.

Men covet youth and beauty. Accept that. That is why you wear makeup and dye your hair. Most women refuse to notice what is directly in front of their faces. They believe what they want to believe just as I did when I was 4. You're not 4 anymore. Reality is warm, come on in for a dip.

Due to conformity or the way that a culturally Marxist society hollows out the mind, women now ape male behaviors. They pretend to want what we want. Now they reportedly covet youth and beauty too. Nice!

Well, this would be acceptable if they actually believed it. Only they are still women. They crave men with wealth and status. This results in a FUBAR situation for them.

For the most part, wealth and status are seldom present in the young and the beautiful. Of course there are celebrity exceptions, but generally wealth and status come with age. Tell me, if women are so much better than men why do so many of them re-engineer themselves to copy our desires? Doing so leads to a great deal of female misery.

Let me now restate Chapin's Rhodium Law of Human Behavior:

***the more one's actual life conflicts with one's biological
nature, the more unhappy he or she increasingly becomes.***

If you are a woman and you decide to defy your instincts in order to sleep
with younger men who do not give a damn about you, and are unlikely to ever fall
in love with you, then agony is the **expected** resulted. All-too-often, as
pharmaceutical sales suggests, torment is exactly what occurs.

I know of few single women in my age bracket who are **not** miserable. That
my mood does not match theirs is a major obstacle to me successfully working
alongside them. Their pervasive distress makes them unlikely to complete tasks
and also to be generally disinterested in the affairs of children.

Getting to know women in their forties has made going my own way a very
simple endeavor. It makes it easy to have no regrets! Most of the women I have
gone out with in the last four years (42 to 46) were almost exactly my age. I find it
impossible to sustain any kind of emotional arousal with these individuals let alone
physical arousal. Their bodies are regrettable.

Often they laugh to me about how they don't work out and don't enjoy
exercise. They are "too busy." Needless to say, I do not find their comments
amusing. These women are more like peers than lust objects. For the most part,
unless the woman is in fabulous shape, I am only attracted to women who are
younger than me. This renders my situation unsolvable.

It's worse than that. I categorically clash with the present time period.

The other day I happened to see, for the twentieth time, the film *Conan the
Barbarian*. It is from 1982 and I realize now that it is the embodiment of my
sexuality. Arnold Schwarzenegger mates with three different females during its
action. All of the scenarios surrounding these women meet my criteria for sublime
interaction.

First, when he is a gladiator slave, he is bred to "the finest stock." A
superlative female is brought into his cell. Conan cloaks her and discourages the
dregs outside from watching them copulate. What a guy! He then lays her down on
the bed and fills the order. I have no criticism whatsoever of their synergy. Should
I ever be jailed it is my hope that the jailers use me for the same purpose.

The second female he mates with is a witch. Well, that is disappointing, but
she is incredibly fit and demands that Conan have sex with her in exchange for
information. I approve of this. If you want to get action you have to give action. It
was a poetic scene. Sure she scared the hell out of him, but it's the body that

counts. Moreover, the male as a value item element behind their interplay must have triggered many a feminist. Then again, no feminist would ever watch *Conan* in the first place. Crom!

Valeria is his main interest. She was the third and most important babe in the movie. While not as attractive as the other two in my jaded opinion, she is incredibly brave and loyal. As a bonus, she knows right from wrong which is unthinkable in an age of cultural Marxism. Valeria recognizes that evil exists. This makes her the mental superior of every college aged female in 2016. Of the film's main villain, she observes,

> *To the hell fires with Thulsa Doom. He's evil; a sorcerer who can summon demons. His followers' only purpose is to die in his service. Thousands of them.*

Preach on sister! They do not make women like that nowadays.

Valeria's love for Conan is passionate. She is one of the few thieves in history who would not meet the definition of "low company."

In short, *Conan the Barbarian* IS my sexuality which gives you an excellent understanding as to why I am going my own way.

My sexuality is as out of vogue today as my political opinions. I am repulsed by the idols of our age.[19] To say I am "vanilla" is an understatement. I am not very open-minded sexually. I am a heterosexual. I do not believe in diversity when it comes to sexual attraction. I lust women and that's it. I don't want to experiment. I do not wish to pretend I am a woman or have "equal roles in the bedroom." Such a notion is repugnant. Just ask Conan.

I do not want to boss a woman around or dominate her unless it is in the privacy of our boudoir. On that score I am surprisingly flexible and kindly as I am a giver.

Yet none of my Conan-esque sexual fantasies are acceptable now. I will sum up my sexual desires with a simple phrase: *conquer and own.* I am like Daffy Duck, "Mine! Mine! Mine!" I do not believe in sharing. What's mine is mine. Cucks, fuck off, leave the way you came in.

If a woman acts too communal in my presence I treat her the same way I would Bernie Sanders. I do not want a proportional share of a female. I want her all to myself. I want to conquer and own.

Should a girl have the smell of the bucks all over her, I promptly abandon her. I have been that way since I was 16. That part of me will never change. *"It's so 1950"* to be jealous of a woman nowadays. Well, too bad. The joke is on them because I only act in a possessive manner if I really like a girl which means I hardly ever display such behaviors. Actually caring about them is wholly out of place in an androgynous society. Therefore, I would rather flee the battlefield than function as a metrosexual in a relationship.

It's a gynocentric culture. Women rule! Men drool. Poppycock.

What I know for certain is that I find female dominance repulsive. I become instantly irate if a woman tries to order me about in an intimate setting. It completely alienates me to have a supervisor around when the lights are off. Indeed, during my two most recent encounters, I specifically told them ahead of time, as a disclaimer, that they would be wise not to make too many demands of me in the heat of the moment. I would probably "shut down" which is an understatement.

The first time I began to recognize the perils of our progressive age was in 1998. I had two separate incidents in which the women tried to administer our sexual maneuvers. I reacted very negatively. On both occasions, I got up and told them to get out. Both contacted me later but I did not return their phone calls.

I'll be your huckleberry, but only for cash money. In my free time I want to live as a free man. I would make a very poor masochist indeed, and an even worse citizen in the ~~progressive~~ regressive age.

Chapter 6: NO BOUNDARIES

Those who are obsessed with others do so out of a need to hide things from themselves.

To avoid criticism say nothing, do nothing, be nothing.
                                        —Aristotle

One of the most disappointing aspects of being a devout heterosexual is realizing that there is a vast expanse between your average male and female when it comes to personal boundaries and space. Men are more apt to stay in their lane while the boundaries of your average female are about as structured as a Friday night in a Brazilian favela.

Women habitually samba back and forth between their own lives and those of friends, intimates, associates, and even complete strangers. No intrusion is unwarranted in their minds. They don't like to study, but they do LOVE to gossip. However, only one of these is a legitimate enterprise.

Women will manufacture false information and then trade it for pounds of gibberish. This mash of blarney is then forged into either character assassination and/or an entertaining story. It is then marketed with the heading, "did you hear?"

If they are caught engaging in such diabolical activities they will take no responsibility for what they have done. Most likely they will cry, and then blame you for making the truth known. A woman's tears are a 911 call that will reach the ear of any white knight within a two mile radius.

Women also will reveal intimate details about themselves and others in the most bizarre settings. They do so with such regularity that I often stare at them and wonder, "What the fuck is wrong with you?"

Quite a bit as it turns out, but *Guidetopsychology.com* explains what the term boundaries means:

> *By definition, a boundary is anything that marks a limit.*
> *Psychological limits define personal dignity. When we say,*
> *"You just crossed a line," we are speaking about a*
> *psychological limit that marks the distinction between*
> *behavior that does not cause emotional harm and behavior*

that causes emotional harm...Boundaries, unlike
psychological defense mechanisms, are conscious and
healthy ways to protect ourselves from emotional harm.[20]

Boundaries are also essential when interacting with others. You stay over there, I will stay over here. That is the way I live my life. If you and I don't have a direct problem then we don't have any problems. How you differ from me is not germane. What you think is none of my business. I am not the thought police. I actually feel bad when I give others unsolicited advice, yet sometimes I cannot help myself.

Most women do not honor boundaries. They lack all sense of self-control in this regard. They do whatever they want and stomp across any marker that they wish. Our gynocentric society forbids criticism of the ornate sex. This means there are no limits or rejoinders that follow many of the outrageous things they do or say.

The feminist revolution and the cultural Marxism spewed by the media and the academy have negated any chance of social pressure modifying their characters. There are no checks and balances. Our worship of women represents a marked departure from history. Our ancestors knew better than to treat women like gods. They comprehended that a female was just another form of human. Saying that a woman is no better than anyone else is blasphemy in 2016...but it remains the case. Much that once was...is now lost.[21]

A woman's "need to know" can liquate a barbed wire fence. There's no stopping a snoopy female. That the word "snoopy" is used instead of "psycho" is also a tribute to how gynocentric our society is. What do you call someone who has no boundaries? You should term them a dangerous anti-social personality, but now we dub them "normal."

In my personal life I have witnessed my trust and comfort be eroded by actions and statements that certain women definitely *did not have to make.*

Too much curiosity and mindless opinion kills both romance and even friendship. I do not exist as a vehicle by which to deliver information. If I do not wish to share something with you then that is my decision and mine alone. Questioning and harassing me over that decision only alienates me further. Zero boundaries are another and a major reason why I am a man going his own way.

In relationships, I often demarcated a zone for no entry, yet the women I dated tried to break into the area with tanks and flamethrowers. Recently, I told a girl that I was upset about something but did not want to talk. A second later my phone rang. I stared at it in the manner I would an alien invasion. What the hell was she doing? I answered it despite my better judgment. I had a serious problem but I suddenly had a second one after this idiot started ordering me about as if I was her valet. That they do such things is amazing. No obstacle to their power can be permitted. Obviously, restoring one's attraction after such encroachments is an arduous task.

Porous lines between self and others renders intimacy impossible. How can you trust someone who shouts over a PA what you tell them? I cannot. Keeping secrets is always promised, but these vows are quickly forgotten if the girl feels the need to dish. This happens whenever a woman hears something that another woman would die to hear. The control-Dish button is then hit.

Whenever a romanticant of mine reveals that she has been confabulating about "us" to her ~~friends~~ co-competing parasites I writhe in disgust. I want to ask, "So then I'm the enemy then? I'm the person you sell out? I thought I was your significant other? Some *us*."

A humorous conversation I have had a thousand times with women occurs after they first approach me to ask if I want to hear something wild. I say sure. *Something Wild* was a great movie. They then tell me not to tell anyone and to promise that I won't.

I say, "I am a MAN OF HONOR™. I won't tell anyone. Besides no one asks me anything or cares much about my opinion."

"Okay, so you're not going to tell anyone then? Promise?"

Didn't I already answer that question? The term "MAN OF HONOR™" bounces off their ears like ancient Aramaic. They have no idea what it means. Their thoughts are limited to the moment. Honor is not fleeting. It is long-term and endures. Thus, its implications are lost on them. That I would, due to a vow, refrain from putting myself at subsequent advantage at their expense is a possibility so unlikely they do not even deem it worthy of consideration.

There used to be a phrase when I was a kid that was applied to those who did not respect boundaries. It was "mind your own business." I still remember a school psychologist that I worked with years ago who used the term as an acronym. She would frequently shout down the halls, "Jimmy, MYOB!"

Fortunately that phrase has seldom been directed at me since I was a child. It's a point of pride and in keeping with my worldview to mind my own business. MYOB is a powerful expression of the libertarian personality.

The times in which I stuck my nose somewhere it did not belong are very embarrassing memories for me. I remember the unpleasant times when I violated another person's space as well. This usually happened when I was drinking. I would end up telling some guy what to do about some dilemma in which he definitely did not ask for my opinion. That was unacceptable. Generally, I called the next day to apologize.

Currently, I face an uncertain future so I have asked some of the fellows who now live off the internet—e.g. Davis Aurini, Matt Forney, and Aaron Clarey—rather intimate financial details. It bothers me to do this. I explain to them that my interest in them is not personal, but, rather, I wish to stare into the fate which awaits me. I use them as palantírs. They help me adjust for my upcoming dilapidated state.

Yet my attitude towards personal space is not shared by most women. In fact, it is shared by almost no woman I have ever known. Too many have displayed no scruples when it comes to gossip acquisition. Their entire existence could be summarized by the title of an excellent film about the GDR: *The Lives of Others*.

There seems to be no limit to what they think they are entitled to know.

I recall laughing hysterically after a girl once asked me on a date how much money I made. I answered, "Ah, that's kind of personal. Don't you think it's rude to ask people personal questions?" She didn't. I never saw her again.

My legendary friend Dianabol had a similar experience. An ex asked him repeatedly about his income. Finally, he said "what's your fax number? I'll send you my W2." Not getting the joke, she then gave him her fax number. We still laugh about this story.

One of the consequences of having a feminized society is that words like rude and polite have lost their meaning. Everyone is their own talk show host. They want to know everything. I do not even look at my Facebook feed anymore. If I see any more pictures of sub-average women striking model poses for selfies I will have to terminate my account.

All of my readers have had girlfriends who went through their phones to see who they called and who was on their contact list. They have also had them rummage through cupboards looking for who knows what in the never-ending pursuit of incriminating material. Why do such persons go to such lengths to guarantee their own unhappiness?

The two most striking autobiographical examples of this occurred with my ex-wife Shannon and my ex-girlfriend Erica. Erica turned out to be a real over-achiever. She later went into the stripper business. Luckily, she never asked me for any back pay for the champagne room shows I witnessed in our apartment.

With Shannon there were many episodes. An early one occurred when I was working late at the drug store one night in 1994. I had grad school classes the next day so I planned on just going home after my shift. She wanted to sleep over which was fine with me. Shannon came by the store and I loaned her the keys to my apartment so she could let herself in before I got off. An hour later I arrived to find a crying Shannon. I thought something had happened. I looked to see signs of a break-in. Instead, I met the eyes of a monster. She howled, "You still have pictures of your ex (Erica)! Why do you still have them?

I looked around the room in confusion. "What are you talking about? I see no pictures."

Shannon disappeared into my bedroom which contained only a mattress and a closet. She came back carrying a cigar box in which I kept pictures. "They're in here!"

"Well what are you doing in there? Mind your own business you sneak! I trusted you and you rewarded me by ransacking the place."

She had no answers but stared at me with a hateful look. A few months later we were in her parent's basement and there were pictures of her college boyfriend in a frame. Of course, she never destroyed those nor would she. Typical.

I sat down on the couch appalled. I had lent her my keys so she would not have to wait around outside. That was considerate. Shannon then raped my trust. She used my kindness as a cloak for her Stasification of my apartment. I almost expected to find bugs in the phone and wires in the wall afterwards. She had no boundaries and was willing to cry, lie, and burglarize as a way to find out as much about me as she could.

For my part, I never did destroy those pictures of Erica. I still have them. I sometimes disparage the past, but I always acknowledge it. I do not believe in Sovietizing history.

In that same apartment, a year before in July of 1993, my relationship with Erica had come to an end. She was livid on that day after moving all of her stuff out. Before leaving, she told me to call her so I could hear all about her "new dudes." Dudes as in plural!

The next morning I lay in bed. Thin embers of sun illuminated the room. I had gone out the night before but awoke to some sort of disturbance. What was it? I then saw Erica enter the bedroom and demonstrate about like a feminist at a slut rally.

"Erica? What are you doing here?"

She was furious. She shouted, "Where is she?"

"Who?"

"The girl who was here last night."

"There was no girl here last night."

"Yes there was. I saw two wine glasses in the sink. Who was here with you?"

"Oh, Dave was over and we had port before we went out."

There was then a pause. She psychoed down. My story had the odor of truth. Dave and I were broke so we often drank before we went out. Erica sat down on the bed and began weeping.

One thing really bothered me though. "Erica?" I said.

"What?"

"How did you get in here? I latched the dead bolt last night."

She began to cry hysterically but said nothing.

I got up and walked into the front room. She had ripped the screen off an open window and climbed in. I came back holding the screen. I had no idea how to fix it. My bank account contained 80 dollars. I ended up keeping the window shut until the lease expired.

It was the last time I saw Erica. I should have called the cops.

The philosophical tenet that *the ends do not justify the means* is not a conviction held by most women. Whatever it takes to procure material or have their desires met will be initiated. No violation is below them. The lines between sacred and profane are blurred. Their creed is **By Any Means Necessary** when it comes to spoiling themselves. The law will not punish them. Our greater society automatically labels criticism as "sexism." Should you describe their violations of space you will be branded a misogynist. I am done caring about any of it.

Leo Tolstoy understood the ornate sex. He wrote:

When I have one foot in the grave I will tell the truth about
women. I shall tell it, jump into my coffin, pull the lid over
me, and say, 'Do what you like now.'[22]

I am still alive but I will tell the truth until the day I die.

I have had many jobs. At all of them I was habitually aware of my female coworkers' personal lives. I never asked about their families or their love objects. I never wanted to know any details, but somehow I always heard them. I knew their children's names. The same for their husbands and friends. I was familiar with their vacation spots. I heard what food they liked, and even where they went on the weekends. For reasons I cannot fathom, I was exposed to all of it.

This was principally due to their having a faulty sense of boundaries. That "work" is a different setting from "home" is not something that most of them understand or respect. Everywhere they go they are still there so why don't they have the right to talk about themselves? The female supervisors never minded. They engaged in the prattle and gossip during work hours along with the rest of the crew.

Was it not selfish of me to expect them to focus on task completion? No, but I believe that many of my female peers took my work ethic as a personal affront. Was I trying to make them look bad? The job really was all about them. I must have had it all wrong.

That what you do at home is not what you do at work is a revolutionary idea to them. To me it is natural and non-controversial. They kept it real by really fixating on themselves. I will not say much more about this as *Working with Women* will be a separate book.

Yet I have always believed in the words Robert Greene wrote in *On Power* concerning this subject: **"Keep your friends for friendship, but work with the skilled and competent."** Absolutely correct.

Greene's words wildly crash against the matriarchy. Women form cliques wherever they go. This is particularly true at work. I was once advised, in 2004, that I should have lunch in the principal's conference room because they "talked about" whoever wasn't there. I told the lady who gave me the advice "to let them talk." I did not give a damn about their opinion. This deeply shocked her. What she did not realize was that while I labored at an elementary school I was not a student at the elementary school. Anyone who feels that they have to "talk about others" has nothing going on in the confines of their brain.

We see this perpetually on display with *googling*. Women do it addictively. I have heard the sinister habit defended with frivolities like, "oh, come on, don't you always look up the people that you meet?"

No. No I do not. I have boundaries and am psychologically healthy. Googling is for the psychologically unwell. I do not treat strangers as enemies upon whom I need to spy.

In the dating context, the excuse that most women use is that they googled you "to make sure you are not a criminal." This is utter subterfuge. First, if they found out someone was a criminal then it would fulfill many of their greatest fantasies. It would be a baby maker, not a deal breaker.

Second, what they actually want to do is find out all about you beforehand. They want to interact with you from a position of superiority rather than as an equal.

This is bunkum. Intimacy should be established gradually. It does not result after a sudden maelstrom of information, and much of it distorted in my case. Instead of listening to a person and getting to know them, these women jump the queue and use feelz as opposed to experience to make decisions.

I always want to ask them about their fabulous intuition. If they were truly intuitive souls could they not divine something about a person without the aid of an electronic device? One would presume so. What is so disturbing—and something I have witnessed personally—is that what they "discover" becomes more real to them than what they actually participate in on a daily basis.

Due to a complete lack of boundaries I was despised at my job. A malignant narcissist googled me and then lied to the others about what she found. Nobody bothered to look into the matter. They just believed her. After all she did have a vagina.

Thanks to female out-grouping, my co-workers readily bought that I was guilty of all sorts of things. To my knowledge, not a single person quoted an actual word that I ever said in over 3,600 videos. If you are a dedicated ignoramus, responding to actual statements is unnecessary. Far more valid than facts are your emotional impressions after coming across titles which "triggered" you.

The idiots concluded that because I own guns and shoot them at the range that I was some kind of felon. The Second Amendment was either something they had not heard of (a real possibility!) or they thought that "the right of the people to keep and bear Arms, shall not be infringed" applies to only to the police.

Their immense intelligence reliably informed them…that I was not a member of the police. Hence, what was I doing firing a gun at a range? Why was I frequently laughing instead of crying as they would have done? Had I been a good person I would have felt shame and guilt upon pulling the trigger. Fuck those imbeciles.

Anyone with even a modicum of knowledge comprehends that most people do not suddenly become outlaws at age 46. I have never been arrested for any crime. I have never been questioned about a crime by the police, and I also have never received any citations for moving violations or illegal parking. No matter.

As progressive dipsticks, they felt like it was true...which provided them with justification for destroying me. I was not a member of the clique so no one had to feel bad about it. Besides, acting in a malicious manner entertained them.

Hearing my actual voice utter impieties like "having a vagina doesn't mean you won the lottery," and "you're special...just like everyone else" amounted to an armed assault. My views detonated all their fabricated feelings of superiority. I was an enemy. I blocked progress.

What their violent reaction really demonstrated is just how little criticism they were ever subjected to and how morbidly obese their egos are.

Had I stuck to writing and never founded a video channel, things would have gone easier for me. None of them are capable of reading unassigned materials. If it is not on TV or in common gossip then they have no idea what it is. I recall one of them telling me, a few years ago, that she had never heard of Muammar Gaddafi. I told her he was the President of Libya. Libya did not ring any bells either. I dropped the subject.

Luckily, I IQ tested out of snoopery. It would be inconceivable for me to google my co-workers and then harass them about what I found. If I did search them, which would never happen, but if I did, I would have the wisdom to keep my lapse in boundaries hidden from the general public.

Women have no such shame. Over the last few years I have gotten used to several harpies scowling at me out of the blue and then giving me the cold shoulder. They are THE SHUNNERS. I suppose they think using such a tactic is very sophisticated. It isn't. Shunning is a behavior that 5-year-old females exhibit. Should we not expect these persons to grow up? Yes we would, but they never did.

By the end of my career I cared little about any of them. I was just there to work...which made me a bad employee. The shunning had no effect because I had no desire to talk to most of my peers in the first place. Their personalities were about as exceptional as water coming from the faucet.

What they did to me is known as indirect aggression. I call it cowardly aggression as not one of the yellow-bellies would ever approach me outside of work to say a thing. None of these women are better than a single man I know. No male would stoop to such a low level.

I was always left wondering, "What exactly have I done to you?"

Nothing. Yet they think that anyone who criticizes "women" is actually criticizing them. In-group affiliation seems to be their only true affiliation. My failure to celebrate women in my videos meant that I "hated them," but the only behavioral evidence we have is that *they hated me*. My honor precludes ever treating **anyone** in the same manner.

Some of them probably had never heard a smidgeon of criticism in their entire lives and simply hearing female inadequacies uttered aloud devastated them psychologically. They may have despaired, "You mean we are merely human?" Yes, and not the cream of the homo sapiens either. More like the skim milk.

They believe that "real men" are the ones who let women push them around. Wrong! Such fellows are bugs, not men.

What I learned from this scourging is that turning on someone for only just reasons, as opposed to trivial or phantom reasons, is a male characteristic. Females often turn on others based on whim. Contrary to what the social justice warriors say, when you have very real privilege in society—as women do—there is no cause to ever "check" it.

Women outgroup others should the mood strike them. I take the making enemies very seriously. The ornate sex does not. Women value conformity and will go along with whatever the herd is doing. They have hive minds. They may bully others based on a friend's recommendation or out of a desire to "support them." There is no penalty for their spontaneous harassment. When it is identified, they will then play the victim and put out the ruse that you did something to deserve their irrational treatment.

I did not classify most of the women I knew as friends or enemies. They were simply people I worked with. I put aside my personal views in the pursuit of a greater goal…production.

Googling me and its accompanying vendetta was not something the women I worked with should have done in the first place. It never occurred to them that just because you can do something does not mean that you should. They simply could not control themselves. They cannot resist creating their own apartments in hell.

Yet I still wonder what dysfunction possesses them whenever I hear that one of them "looked someone up" online. I want to shake them and demand, "Why do you have so little self-respect that you brag about being deranged?"

They do it because they can and there are no societal repercussions.

Are the hobbies and political interests of your peers any of your business? No, end of story.

Should one ask a woman "what's up with the all the googling?" One will immediately hear the Chapin Theory of Female Crypsis articulated. They will announce, "I never google people and guys do it too."

Bollocks to all that.

Out of all the reasons cited in this book for why I have gone MGTOW I suspect that the "no boundaries" issue in the biggest.

Whenever I am with a woman I feel as if they want way too much from me. The space gets narrower and narrower. It's as if I have to keep a verbal torch at all times in order to wave them back and maintain my sense of self.

In 2000, my then girlfriend said to me, "I just want to fold you up and place you inside of me." I was completely repulsed. I told her that was the sickest thing I ever heard. To her, having no boundaries was best practice. To me, it created a gender segregated brown land I never want to enter.

Chapter 7: Pet Semetary

Every parting gives a foretaste of death, every reunion a hint of the resurrection.
> —Arthur Schopenhauer

My sun sets to rise again.
> —Robert Browning

After my MGTOW moment in 2002 everything was recolored. I began to realize that what I wanted was not what I thought I wanted. What was I doing constantly auditioning with people I don't really like and don't get along with?

My marriage ended unhappily in 1996. Afterwards, if I had women on any sort of pedestal it was not much of one. Whatever place I had them in was lowered by a few notches with each passing year.

By 2002, I was both suffering and benefiting from Red Pill malaise. The thrill of the chase was fading but I had not really found anything else. I was still heavily addicted to women but no longer had marriage on my mind. If marriage was not a consideration, and I was no longer a mad dog after sex, then what exactly was I doing with them?

A lot and a little as it turns out. I came to the conclusion that women would always be a short-term pleasure/pain in my life. I stopped worrying about the future. My tolerance for superficial, irritable personalities became limited. My heart just was not in it as it was previously. It was the physical connection that kept me in my relationships and that alone.

The variation in me did not strike me as severe, but I changed far more than I realized. Just a short time after digesting the Red Pill, I reencountered two women I used to date who suddenly decided they were interested again. I would follow suit wouldn't I? They assumed that if they were amenable to continued relations then I would be as well. They assumed incorrectly. They must have been surprised to see the man that I contorted into in just a few years.

My conversion, and the girl's responses, reminded me of the movie *Pet Semetary* wherein a man buries his dead wife in a haunted Indian burial ground.

Her life is restored, but she is not the person he remembers. Happily he hugs her. He's so glad she is with him again. She responds to his embrace by stabbing him viciously with a knife.

Well there were no crimes or dramas in my case, but a girl I went out with when I was 31 suddenly began emailing me in 2004. She wrote, "Are you the same Bernard Chapin who wrote 'Sex in the Zeroes' online?"

I was. It was penned for the now defunct *Toogoodreports.com*.

"Do you remember me?" she typed. "It's Melanie. Only now I'm going by the name Lanie."

I responded in the affirmative. I remembered her loose and free body as well. Lean with adiposity in all the right places she managed to capture my affections for at least a month. I knew her as Melanie, but I would have to call her "Lanie" this time around. Name alteration is a very strange decision for a 28-year-old to make.

I avoided calling her on the phone. We messaged back and forth a few times. Ala internet date, I agreed to meet her out on a Saturday afternoon. We decided on the Twisted Spoke which was close to both of our apartments. We met out front and got seated up on the roof next to the skeleton riding a motorcycle. To her, the bones were scenery. To me, they were symbolic.

I was pleased to see that Melanie still looked good. A few pounds heavier sure, but she was never overweight to begin with.

We were there for an hour and it was about as stimulating as a moisturizer commercial. I remembered that previously she only really had a personality when she drank, and now she had ice tea in front of her. Lanie talked about herself a great deal. I had flashbacks about two years before when I would sit on the phone listening to the trivialities of her life. I, in turn, said very little.

In the midst of making verbal notes for her memoir, Lanie tried to recapture my attention. She mentioned how passionate we were in the spring of 2001. I was really into her, she said. That was rather condescending but I made no comment.

Lanie then asked about the World War II book she had given me. Did I still have it? Yes, I did. Was I seeing anyone? No, I was not. Was she involved with someone else? I don't know as I knew not to ask the question.

Foreshadowing my turbulent vocational future, she asked if the articles I wrote would get me into trouble at work. I did not think they would (I was wrong).

That was about the only non-small talk we engaged in. Lanie never said that we should try again, but she went on for a while telling me how unworthy most of her suitors were. I felt so bad for her! To be honest, I do not think she said much more than that. It was all fluff.

Previously I had been amused by her Hitlerian table talk. Now I found her conversation unbearably self-absorbed and tedious. She was boring. Of course, I could have overlooked all of that had it not been for one issue…the past.

While Melanie fit my criteria for physical attraction, I was still carrying a grudge and never made mention of it. We did have a bit of an intense relationship. She was right and I was really digging her. After all, she was 25. It seemed as if she really liked me, but she did nothing to preserve what we had. In fact, she liquidated it.

The only reason I stopped seeing her was that after I came back from my 10 year reunion at John Carroll she told me on the phone she could not see me the following weekend.

"Why not?" I asked. "Even Sunday? What are you doing?"

"Social things. I'm busy."

"You're doing 'social things'? What does that mean?"

"You know, social things."

"Fine, goodbye." I hung up the phone. What the hell did that mean? A new guy? Lesbian sleepover? What?

I soon found out.

The next weekend came and I was out with the fellows at the Taste of Randolph festival. We did this every year. It was one of the best street fairs and I always seemed to do quality work.

While standing there finishing a beer with Dianabol, I happened to see Melanie pass by with a guy who was 10 years older than me. His beard was actually gray. Amid the throng of people, they did not notice me standing next to one of the tents. What was worse was that Melanie and this Wily Old Gentleman were holding hands. And I thought our relationship had progressed quickly! Maybe this was no new acquaintance. Perhaps she had been going out with him for even longer than she had with me. Needless to say, seeing them together made me sick. I'm no Jeb Bush. I don't do the cuck thing. I was in no in a hurry to ever see her again.

I said nothing and let them pass. Later I was grateful. It is rare with dating, when one can directly witnesses evidence that provides closure. What a bitch. When the loving couple walked by I was done with her. This girl, with all her intellectual pretensions, was nothing but an upperclass skank. Good riddance!

Now she was "Lanie" and I was sitting with her at the Twisted Spoke. Yet she had already been closed out. This was a formality. A zombie's raid on history. I thought of that display at Randolph Street but did not mention it.

Lanie had to be shocked by the Bern she had before her. I presented a complete lack of emotionality. What happened to the old expressive dupe who took her to the Hudson Club three times? He was dead. Zed's dead baby.

I stared at her through my sunglasses despite it being an overcast day. This was an easy opportunity. Instant intimacy! The groundwork had been laid two years before this date. I was sure that I could have had some sort of physical relationship with her and very soon at that. Was it worth it?

I thought about it during that hour. No. Unforgiven.

Apart from her monstrous hooter-mcgooters I had no enthusiasm whatsoever. Her body failed to motivate me. Honor before sex. I paid the check, shook her hand, and said, "Farewell." She did not email again.

In my twenties, I would have agreed with the statement "honor before sex." "Yes!" I would have shouted. My behavior though would have shown that I had not internalized such beliefs.

By 2004, I was a completely different person than the trim jockey Melanie had known in 2001. Females liking me remains somewhere on my top 100 list of desires to this day, but it sure as heck is not in the top 10.

Now I live by this code: **Loyalty is a reciprocal proposition.**

There will be no white knighting in my future or any chasing of the past.

Three years later I passed "Lanie" in a Kinko's. I recognized her, said nothing and kept on walking. Fuck her.

A similar incident occurred in 2006. The man the girl rediscovered was not the fellow she used to know. It also started in 2001. Five years earlier Frankie told me about a girl he worked with who "totally loved history."

"Really?" I said…astounded. "Is she good looking?"

"Yeah, she's 24 and stacked."

"No way. That sounds like a fairy tale. Give me her email man."

"Ah, I'll ask her if it's okay first." Frankie was wise to do that otherwise his employer could fire him for sexual harassment.

Frankie spoke to her and she was fine about me contacting her. He gave me her home email address. Her name was Gayle. For about two months we zipped back and forth, mostly about history and *her* life. In case you are wondering, Gayle did not know much about history. She knew something about the Civil War and that was about it. History was not part of her life in the way it is mine (obviously).

No worries. I kept asking her out anyway. She kept delaying me. It was 2001 so we swapped *low-resolution* pictures. I felt sure that Gayle liked me, but I never got a "yes" when it came to meeting.

Around Thanksgiving, I gave up. I stopped sending her emails and desisted in responding to hers. I am not an attention providing accoutrement for a woman's self-concept. A pen pal was not what I was looking for. Gayle was cute and promising, but if she did not want to date I couldn't make her. It was just business. I did not take it personally.

However, in February of 2002, Gayle emailed me unexpectedly. She wrote, "I have to meet you." Now you're talking! I was pleased to hear from her. The more prospects the better. She did not bother with "what's up" or "how are you." Gayle was typing my tune.

Frankie gave me some background information. He told me that Gayle had been going out with someone in the fall. She did not want to cheat on him at the time, but now it was academic. They had broken up. I was the utility infield player. She had kept me in reserve. I was slated to bat for the pitcher. Hey, I didn't mind in the least.

That Friday night we met at John Barleycorn's in Wrigleyville on the second floor. Due to the primitive digital camera technology available at the time, I was not entirely sure what she looked like. I did know that I approved of her body which was more than enough for me.

I saw a girl walk by and before I knew it Gayle started groping me. I had not even recognized her yet. I hugged her back. It seemed like a wonderful moment. We went outside and made out in the parking lot for 20 minutes. I did not take her home or even try to which pleased me. This girl was one that I really wanted. Patience was a given.

We began talking on the phone all the time. We dated twice a week. Things progressed quickly. Gayle used to complain about the wave of manginas and non-masculine men proliferating throughout society. I proved a receptive audience for her observations. Making fun of those freaks is great conversation!

Gayle seemed to appreciate me and I appreciated her right back. We had a great month. I had no complaints. I took her to all my favorite places. It was very passionate. I even convinced myself that there was an element of fate involved (oh God) in our courtship. In those days, I could delude myself about anything.

In the midst of our Adult Swim, Gayle called to say that we could not go out any longer. I was stunned. She was speaking with a new voice and I hated it. What came over her and what the hell was she talking about?

Gayle announced dramatically, "This is happening too fast. I don't want to feel all those things again. It's too soon for me to get involved with someone. I don't want to fall in love."

I had not read much in the way of pickup artist literature at the time, and did not know what a shit test[23] was, but what she was doing certainly met the definition of it. Had I read the *Mystery Method* or *The Game* I would have played the outburst differently.

Instead of seeing her words as a female rapport break, I chose to believe her. Since I was a man of my word I assumed that she a woman of her word. What a juvenile assumption. Asinine ideas like that proved that I had yet to understand women at all.

Her words shocked me. Flabbergasted, I called her a fucking coward. I said, "If you quit now you're going to be quitting for the rest of your life." She agreed with me but I was not listening. I had made the mistake of taking her seriously and treating her as my equal (!). I figured that her mind was made up and could not be changed. I did not bother trying.

I had royally failed her shit test. I raged some more and then hung up the phone. Gayle did not call back and that was that. The situation was not unheard of in those days—a girl acting against their own interests.

The whole thing did not bother me for long. I was a worker and in those days it was not hard to procure new women. No case of one-itis lasted very long. Sadly, none of the new girls were 24 though, but about a month later I had largely forgotten about her.

Gayle happened to live about two blocks from me. Thus, six months later I ran into her on the street. I could not pretend like I did not recognize her as she practically bumped into me at the corner of Pine Grove and Patterson. I gave her a big smile.

"How are you Gayle?"

She gave me a pouty look and feigned disgust.

"Oh come on. Come on!" She spat.

"What?"

"Don't act like you want to see me or smile. I know you hate my guts."

"Gayle, I don't hate your guts. Not at all."

"Whatever!" With that she crossed the street.

This was curious. I had no idea what she was talking about. While I did not understand shit tests, by that point I knew how whimsical women were. There was no reason to hate a cat just because she scratched your furniture. It's a cat. Mangling chairs is their nature.

Gayle probably thought I was still pining for her, and just acting when I said hello. Yet I was never in love with her in the first place. She may have been shaken by visual evidence of the fact that she had not ruined my life.

The skitchiness of the encounter made me call Frankie. He was unfazed. "Oh that girl Gayle? You saw her again? Yeah, she's nuts man. You're best off without her. I don't see her at work anymore. She's on a different floor but I do know that she's about to get married."

"What? Married? To the guy she was going out with before me?"

Frankie started laughing. "No, some chuck she just met. It's a 'whirlwind romance' she said. The guy doesn't know her well so she's eager to seal the deal. What a psycho! You're better off without her man."

I was very pleased by this news. Don't Look Back is the way I like to live. "Thanks Frankie. You made my day man. That is hilarious."

After that, I truly forgot about the desperado who formerly went by Gayle. As Morrissey may have sung, "Some girls are sicker than others."

Fast forward four years. In 2006, I was at the St. Michael's Street Fair with Frankie. We kept going to the same events every year and they stayed fun until I was about 40 or so. That particular night was special. One of my favorite bands, Cake, happened to be playing. Before the show, we were having a great time watching the cleavage come and go. We used to call their processions the Boxtrot.

In the midst of the parade, up came Gayle. She grabbed me by the arm. It was déjà vu all over again. I was astounded.

"Hi" she said.

"What's up Gayle." I immediately started giggling when I saw her empty left hand. "Where's your ring? Where's your beau?"

"Oh, we got divorced. It did not last. It's too bad. He really loved me."

I began laughing hysterically. "I'll bet! You didn't want to fall in love with me and then you got married to a complete stranger."

She waved her hand at me. "Oh shut up. Is that what Frankie said?"

Frankie turned around and gazed out into the sea of mini-skirts.

Gayle grabbed my hand. "Do you still have my phone number?"

This bewildered me. "Of course not. I don't call married women."

"Let me surprise you," she said. "I still have yours. Look." Gayle got out her phone and sure enough my number was still on the memory card.

This did not win my approval. "That's so sad. I feel sorry for your husband. You got married and still kept guys cued in the stable."

"Ex-husband," she corrected.

"Whatever."

"Frankie said you had a girlfriend now."

I did not have much respect for Gayle before that day, but now I had none whatsoever. When presented with a charlatan though you might as well have some fun which is what I proceeded to do. "Yes, my girlfriend is my little pup, and she's a great girl to boot."

Actually that was a lie. I did have a girlfriend but she was a total control freak. I could not stand her, but she had the legs of a gymnast. This necessitated keeping my opinions about her personality to myself. Awesome legs always equate with my pride standing down—at least for a few weeks. Apart from my girlfriend's shape I did not have much positive to say about her. She never trusted me even though I gave her no cause for suspicion…before that night.

Gayle tried to get me to leave with her before Cake began to play.

Leave with her? Why? Where were we going? To talk I guessed.

No thanks. That was absurd. Cake was my favorite band and she was just a cluebag who had disrespected me four years earlier. The choice was simple. I ran towards the stage without her.

Gayle found me thirty minutes later. Their set was well under way. I was singing to every lyric on cue with lead singer John McCrae. I cherished most of their songs and the ones that I didn't were still better than anything played on the radio. The guy next to me was doing the same thing. We may have been the only two people in the crowd who were actual fans. We blasted out every song back to back. The sweaty mass pushed into us constantly and it seemed as if I was singing in stereo.

I then felt Gayle bear-hugging my stomach. How she got through the wall of yuppies I do not know. "This sucks," I thought but I kept caroling. Had she not have gotten the quickie marriage/divorce I may have felt differently about her.

Gayle looked okay. She was about 20 pounds heavier than when I knew her in 2002. I believe this is why she asked me if I still lifted weights. She was hoping to make me feel insecure about my appearance in the hopes of matching her own unsure state. It did not work. I kept crooning.

Then the other mega Cake fan took out a marijuana bowl. He stuck it in front of me and nodded. We were brothers now. He nodded as if to say did I want a hit. I didn't. I hate marijuana. Gayle reached out from behind me and took the pipe from him. She toked deeply from it.

I found that riotous. "You know, Gayle, you just keep underwhelming me tonight baby. What a chick!" For the rest of night I called her "Marley" and "ganja sister." When the concert was over Frankie headed back to Lincoln Park to meet Hazel. I was now alone with Gayle.

I told her that I wanted to go home. I asked for her number. She called my phone but said that was not good enough. She insisted on going to my apartment. Gayle said she knew I would not call her so she was not letting me out of her sight.

"Not this time!" she said.

I think Vegas would have given my odds on having sex that night as being 1 to 1. I didn't like those odds. There was something unsavory about this creature. Besides my girlfriend had pommel horse legs. I tried to hustle away without her but she followed me. I simply gave up and resigned myself to her staying for the night. Her body was still sort of interesting, and seeing all those scantily clad women at the street fair had heightened my desire.

We got in a cab and drove off. I figured that this was not a bad situation as between the dope smoking and the mail-order husband, I no longer gave a damn about her. When we got to my apartment—after she was done critiquing the interior, of course—she produced a sorority list of things she wanted me to do to her.

I was too tired for all that and besides I have never been one for meeting expectations. It's bad practice with women. It reduces me to the role of footman. Only manginas care about being "great lovers." Pleasing women never got me anywhere and I was not going to start doing it at the age of 36.

Gayle suddenly pulled a magnetized picture of my girlfriend off the refrigerator. She said with revulsion, "How old is she?"

"36. Just like me."

"Well that's too old for you!"

A nice bit of foreplay there on her part. I agreed, but said we should take a shower first given the nature of the acts she wanted me to carry out. Also, it was July and we had been sweating outdoors for five hours. Additionally, I wanted to get the stench of reefer out of her hair.

Gayle insisted on me scrubbing her down. I went along with that because I'm a flexible and a giver. It was an uplifting experience. After that, we spent about two hours in various embraces before I fell asleep. I woke up the next morning to find her staring at me. She asked me why I wore a condom after she told me not to. I chose not to answer the question.

Then she made me drive her home after I suggested calling a cab. Gayle told me to call her and I did not respond. She would not get out of the car until she forced me to lie and say that I would call her. I never did. I long ago stopped paying dues in the chump-suckers union. She should have asked to see my membership card before taking my services on.

It was *Pet Semetary* all over again. I was not the same man who yelled at her on the phone after I took the red pill. She thought that I still cared about her, but she was wrong. That she so thoughtlessly discarded our previous relationship meant that I had no feelings for her whatsoever. I certainly no longer saw her as an equal. She was a hopetron, and that was it.

If you're chronically confused about a subject (yourself) yet spend every hour obsessing on it, then what does that say about your worth? You have no worth. There are no participation awards given for non-awareness and counter-productive decision-making.

At that time, and even more in the years since, I find that I no longer romanticize women. Nothing they do surprises me. I consider them to be angle-shooters whom you have to watch very carefully during every transaction. I feel like a casino Pit Boss.

Women do not trust me and I no longer trust them. I guess that's equality. They buried the old me and the fellow that busted out of the grave was not the one they remembered. I live my life for myself. I may be a schlep in this world, but in my tiny arena I am field marshal.

Chapter 8: Females Anonymous

If you don't know what you want then how are you not an inferior person?

You can't be friend-zoned if you won't accept friendship in the first place.

First things first. My name is Bernard and I'm a female-aholic. They are never far from my thoughts and I will admit to you that I am in recovery. I have been romancing the curves for 46 years now. I take it day by day, and know that I am only one rambunctious night away from relapse. I use tokens, medallions, and chips to commemorate the time since I have been freed from their hocus-pocus.

Alas, one is never cured of female addiction. Just as I still have dreams in which I am smoking, I still have dreams wherein I am making love to women. Unfortunately, the women are always 25 in these dreams despite my own advancing age. It never changes. This never enhances my sense of well-being.

I cursed the non-reality of the dream plots enough that my unconscious heard me. One night a "love interest" in my slumber actually came out and said she was 39! Yet when I woke up I realized that she still looked like a 25-year-old (with a fabricated age label stamped upon her). I am as resigned to my unconscious betraying me as I am filling up the gas tank. Despite my reservations, nothing more can be done.

What has always saved me is that I have a requited clause in my mental structure. I am the anti-rapist. If a girl doesn't dig me then I don't dig her…period. It does not matter what they look like. If they are not receptive I don't want anything to do with them. If a woman treats me as a pick-up artist treats a woman there will be no ensuing attraction. I am only too ready to believe that they are not interested. Playing hard to get is an illegitimate strategy on their part. I don't want any more challenges. My life is daunting enough.

Despite what they say about mid-life crises, I am as confident and pleased with myself as I have ever been. My self-regard is high. I have excellent skills. I am looking for a side-job at present. I can do just about any kind of paper work and I have 21 years of experience when it comes to kissing up to customers. I am punctual, organized, and efficient which means that most of the female run firms in the United States would purge themselves quickly of my presence. Being a problem solver and a doer makes you an enemy in such jurisdictions.

My self-esteem in relation to women "liking" me though is very low. I do not possess many of the attributes they covet. I'm no criminal and pretending to be a "bad boy" would fool no one. Going your own way makes you realize that the type of people who lust criminals are defective. They don't deserve me or anyone else who has the ability to make a contribution. What kind of inferitrons want to be screwed over? I will let the masochists bathe in their savageness. I choose freedom.

Yet, while I can tell myself all of this, *once a junkie always junkie*. I take it day-by-day but I know I am vulnerable. It does not take much to commission a fantasy in my head. What I look for in a woman is pretty simple: a. non-obesity, b. meet minimal standards for attractiveness, and c. dig me. That is about it so despite my disdain for the whole process of dating, I occasionally run into trouble. My genes ignore my no fraternization order. They can still threaten my autonomy.

When in doubt I simply repeat to myself, "I don't want what I can get." However, what if what I want suddenly appears?

One such case just happened. It ended badly, but you could have guessed that. In the late spring of 2016, a woman appeared—sort of. I will call her Jamie. She was a fan of mine. Jamie lived in another part of the country, a scenic locale. Generally, in my mind, if they are not within 20 miles of me they do not exist.

She began contacting me all the time. I did not take her seriously. I told her she was a player. This made her cry. Jamie then put forth effort to convince me that she wasn't a player. It worked, but my initial diagnosis was accurate. She talked about sex often which is always a turn off unless it involves me. The girl had the smell of the bucks all over her, but for some reason I suspended disbelief.

Soon we were talking on the phone. This meant nothing to her, but I despise that activity. She complimented me to death and really seemed sincere. After about three weeks, Jamie was granted unique status. We talked every day. The back and forth direct messaging on social media was endless.

Yes, I chat with female viewers of mine on facebook or twitter. This is non-remarkable. Usually I flirt with them about their attractiveness. I pay very little attention to these proceedings. Most of the girls are attractive—at least to my rather suspect eyes—and nothing ever comes of it. I give them honest compliments about their bodies or faces. I state valid opinions that are only discolored by my plummeting criteria for female attractiveness.

Each year that I get older, the girls get younger which means there are more of them that appeal to my "male gaze." These viewers seem to like talking to me and there is no dishonor in it as I do not flatter them about their intellects, skills or personalities (unless it is true). Physical compliments though I dole out like condoms at a university.

Jamie texted me all the revealing pictures that women usually send to degenerate addicts of the female form like your recovering narrator. I liked her body. I kept wanting to see more of it. Jamie was well-built and in good shape. Not great shape, but then again I'm no expense paid trip to Santa Monica myself.

This time it was different though.

Jamie is an epic strategist. Jamie mushed she was "so crushing" on me and that we had to meet. This caught my attention. She tried to get me to fly down there for a wedding she had to attend. In retrospect, I think getting me to go to this wedding was the catalyst for her Bernophilic behavior. That's what she really wanted, a date to her friend's ceremony.

I did not realize that and actually looked into flights even though—due to my persecution at work—I had already canceled a trip to Las Vegas for that very same month. I justified it by figuring that it would not hurt to go somewhere new. Having sex with her for three days was also something that I greatly anticipated.

We could not find a flight that was feasible for our timeframe. There was a cheap charter from Thursday to Sunday, but the return flight was too early for her to get me to the airport. The charter was $180. Everything else was $400. I gave up on making it down there for that weekend.

Jamie decided to come up and see me. I accepted her invitation. I was leery at first, but for three weeks she threw herself at me. Genius tactics. While I did not love her, I was undeniably *into* her. I bought into the whole fantasy.

She did/said three things that shattered my defenses. They made me trust her and feel comfortable. Jamie asked about meeting my mother when she came up. Why this impressed me I still do not know. She also said I "was the man she had been dreaming of." Oh God, I'm that dumb? I fell for that? Yep.

The third chump inducing thing was an act. She went out and bought *Escape from Gangsta Island* and *Women: Theory and Practice*. Jamie then took a picture of herself in bed with my books acting as a bra. Yousah! Devious, crafty, and very original. She had a sucker of some sort on the line.

Suddenly, I had developed feelings for her. I wanted to talk her. The dirty parts of the conversation I enjoyed in particular. I mean, she did not have much to say, but for some reason I appreciated connecting with her. What the hell was wrong with me?

Novelty results in fishdom for a man. There was a bigger factor behind my fall though. **I could say whatever I wanted to this girl.** I did not have to hide from expressing a controversial opinion. That was huge. In order to successfully date today's single female, a man must have very bland politically correct ideas (sic). Fellows like me are forever tormented by having to speak through a filter. With Jamie I could talk freely about any topic I pleased. Who knew in 2016 that such liberties were possible?

There were no googling fears. She knew me—not from the gym, not from work—but from my online publications. What could be better than that? I never wanted this to end. This girl had my full attention. The usual stressors and imploders were removed.

Yet Jamie conned me. She wanted my constant attention and she got it. I was a dope. I did not notice that I had developed feelings towards her until it was too late. Why, despite everything I knew, did I respond to these clever stratagems in such a snevie-like way?

Luckily, it was not meant to be. Without getting into personal details, Jamie's attentions to me waned. We still talked and messaged but she started treating me like a friend. All the sex talk faded away. I felt like the mailman delivering a package whenever I texted her.

One day she said that she did not want a relationship but wished to have three days of "fun" at my house. There was nothing wrong with that. For me, it would be cheaper than…well, you know.

Yet telling me you "don't want a relationship" implicitly communicates that I should not care about you. As I knew from past experience, such a request always has unintended consequences.

For such an accomplished general, Jamie had unwittingly left her flanks exposed. With each passing day, I cared about her less. My sexual fantasies no longer included her. Soon, I dreaded our talks. They were all about her…and there wasn't much to tell! She talked about herself endlessly. I found it harder and harder to call.

Jamie considered herself a writer. I wasn't so sure. She was full of self-importance and bogus self-esteem. After being subjected to a ridiculously long monologue one night, I scrawled out a new bon mot:

You'll generally find that anyone who sounds like they
are full of self-esteem has manufactured most of it.

I put that on Facebook and Jamie immediately accused me of talking about her! I denied it and she appeared to accept my explanation. She was right though. There was another bon mot from earlier that week that she inspired:

The first step to enlightenment is realizing that you're not very interesting so there's no point in talking about yourself all the time.

Jamie was a mommy blogger so you can imagine the type of weathered marsupials she was up against in terms of competition. Fourth or fifth grade skills make you stand out when compared to that horde. Mommy bloggers write about themselves and their children. It's insipid but no different than what you will discover should you ever date single mothers. My son, I hope that fate does not befall you!

Fifteen minutes into the first date you will know the names of their children and the trials they are going through. Who the hell cares? Not you, but it is best not to mention it. Otherwise you are just another guy who *doesn't care*…doesn't care about a woman you met a quarter of an hour before.

Jamie made me read her works which I found painful to do. She said (seriously) that she wanted to produce materials that people could read when they were sitting on the toilet. I sit in a chair far away from the bathroom when I work so why was I being subjected to these toiletries?

When I hit the link for one of her "stories" I scrolled down and immediately came across the words "he rubbed my clit."[24] I began cackling. What the hell is that? Why me? I know people post such things at *Penthouse* but they do not consider themselves professional writers. What was this girl thinking about? Yet I skimmed the whole thing out of obligation.

Like the artist in the film *New York Stories* who cannot bring himself to be encouraging to the girl in regards to her talent (she had none), I was hard pressed to say that Jamie's essays/stories were any good. They weren't. She never thought up any new turn of phrase when a cliché would do. Reading it was painful.

Most of my advice was ignored. I told her that no one wanted to read a 3,000 word blog post, and that google had the SEO set for no more than 800 words.

"So," she answered. "The people who want to read it will read it regardless of length. I have loyal fans." Alas, I was not one of them.

What does one say in response to her statement anyway? She hit my constructive suggestion back with feelz? I changed the topic, but that never worked for long. We always came back to her and her jejune emotions.

Jamie also dictated that she did not want me to post any pictures of her to social media from her time spent at the Bern Love Shack. She did not want us to be publicly linked. That was it. This left the impression that she was embarrassed of me.

With that, the spell was immediately broken. I no longer had any feelings for Jamie. She was now just another of the millions of women I find physically attractive. Nothing more.

Jamie had created another *Pet Semetary* situation without knowing it. By telling me that she did not want a relationship she began to erode my interest. Once my admiration begins to decline it soon hits the zero point. In science this is known as the *skankacious principle Axiom*. The less they appear to care about you the less you care about them. For women, the effect is contraindicative. They fall in love with you as soon as your affections dissipate. It's inevitable. Hey man, its science!

The second to last straw was the social media comment, but honestly what turned me off the most was the incessant gerbiling on the phone. Who wants to hear that claptrap? Every time I said something I felt like I was interrupting her. She was a steamroller. Did she even need another person on the line? Couldn't she just save some AT&T minutes by talking to herself alone in a room?

It took about a week, but I no longer felt protective of her. I told her to cancel her trip which she did. We are associates no more and I did not leave any avenue open for future correspondence.

Despite our lack of physical contact, it took me 15 hours to get over her. When I went to bed that night, after our blowout, I seriously thought I might not be able to make an inferno the next day due to sadness. Yet I woke up in my usual morning mood. Nothing was different. I went to the gym, reworked this chapter, turned on the microphone and rolled tide roll!

Of course, I still have her pictures on my phone. There are some sacrifices that you simply cannot ask a man to make.

I'm firmly ensconced in relationship purgatory. What is my final conclusion though? What do I make of the opposite sex?

I believe it is not true that we cannot live without them. I am living without them just fine at the moment. I do think though that going your own way requires accepting that a certain dopamine pathway in your brain will be shut off forever. You will never be as high as you were in the past. The accompanying effect is that you will never be as low either. We're programmed to "lose it" over women. Waylaying those synapses is not a euphoric experience.

Once a man stops worrying about their opinions and judgments you exclude a great deal of balderdash and muppetry from your existence. The interior walls of my home are ugly. They have not been painted in years…and I could not care less. I do not see such things unless a woman shames me into noting them.

I will always be an aficionado of women's bodies. That will never end. It is burned into my biology and will only terminate when the earth is poured over my grave. I'm no longer "in it to win it." I'm in it *to avoid it*. I want to live an intellectual life now, and it is impossible to do that with active neuro-toxins permeating your house.

If enough of us make the same decision we will have power. I consider myself to be invisible to most women, but, as we'll see in the next chapter, that is not really true. I am technically on the injured reserve. I still have the ability to go in and pitch to the weaker part of the order if necessity demands.

Most of the women I worked with could tell that I did not really want to have much to do with them and that occasionally increased either my stature or hatred with them. The ornate sex is cognizant that they do not have much to offer the thinking man.

My final judgment comes from the fauna kingdom. It is a truism that most people believe that the animal women most resemble is the cat. One can readily understand why. Cats are physically beautiful, lithe, and, most importantly, often behave in a passive-aggressive manner.

There is even a book out on the subject called *The Feline Mystique: On the Mysterious Connection Between Women and Cats*. That women have a great affinity for felines there can be no doubt.

Yet I would argue there is a better comparison to be made when it comes to women and the animal kingdom. Yes, the cat is their kin, but, to me, their closest behavioral relation is the Procyon lotor, aka the common raccoon.

The similarities are vast. As with the ornate sex, raccoons are ubiquitous throughout North America. They are everywhere! In malls, in homes, at local businesses and one also comes across them laid out in the street (think *Girls Gone Wild*).

Raccoons are decorous. They are physically enchanting with robust fitness levels and eyes heavily Lancomed. They excel at self-grooming. Every night one sees their kind entering random houses in coats that are practically mink.

In terms of animal cunning, the raccoon is near the apex. Like women, they are extremely crafty, and dedicated to getting as much free stuff as possible. Raccoons mooch all night and despite lacking any prowess in farming, mining or mechanical production, they still manage to maintain a high caloric intake. Their penchant for overeating has even led them to acquire human diseases such as obesity and diabetes. Raccoons are still below the recently acquired 40 percent level of adiposity for your average American female, but give them time. They're ambitious!

They milk Mother Nature along with those who seldom visit their attics for everything they can. They trash residences and silently commit acts of gross destruction while managing to skulk off before justice arrives. The similarities are uncanny.

Raccoons never ring your doorbell and ask to be admitted in the proper way. They have their own plans. Their agenda is never known to you in advance. Your misplaced levels of trust in your own security are all the invitation they need. It's all smoke and duplicity with them.

Procyon lotor has intuition and her intuition leads her to believe what's yours is hers. She needs a place to raise her young and your arrangement with Commonwealth Edison guarantees that none of her offspring will freeze to death. To the raccoon you are the provider she always dreamed of. The raccoon does not care about who purchased your house because she knows after a few years it's going to be hers one way or another. The raccoon knows no boundaries and replaces your valuables with toxic waste.[25]

Like women, this carnivora is an expert survivor. Where you are not is where he or she will be. Their skills at adaptation are formidable. They love objects that men construct, and, once ensconced within them, are notoriously difficult to get out. Think "British at Tobruk" when contemplating how challenging it is to get them to leave on their own. QED.

What would a woman say in regards to this animalian comparison? Chapin's Theory of Female Crypsis applies. The mutually exclusive answers would spew forth quickly. No doubt a loud shriek would be emitted by those gynocrats familiar with the raccoon's ways. They'd bark, "that would never apply to us!" Perhaps a milder "No" would be proffered by those who, out of ignorance, confuse the raccoon with a cuddy little friend they longed to pet as a child.

Thereafter, both parties would labor to show why Procyon lotor is more male than female. "No! That's really you, not us!"

Wrong. "Procyon" should replace "feline" as a way to describe the opposite sex. Regardless, no woman would ever accept this new connection. A cloud of hyper-verbal gobbledygook would rain upon any male who utters it.

Standard. Welcome to a woman's love for dissimulation, shadows and darkness. Traits that would be highly esteemed by your average raccoon.

I will have to leave off here. I have a 5 o'clock Females Anonymous meeting at church that I must attend. I hope the black coffee is fresh.

Chapter 9: MGTOW...Forever!

Always was a sucker for the right cross
Never wanted to go home 'til the last cent was lost
                    —Bob Dylan

The arc of the universe is long and bends towards barbarism.

My worst sexual experience was my second to last. It was eleven years in the making but certainly was a nightmare.

I have always felt a certain lament when a young man tells me he's going MGTOW. I do not want the kid to miss out on all the fun I had. What about the plus/minus statistic? What about all those nights wandering into strange bars and making out with women? That was a sublime time, and it is that reservoir of memories that provides contentment now that I am going my own way.

Yet I cannot deny that my own experiences were lucky. How fortunate I was to miss out on the false allegation mania that millennials have to face today. Not to mention visits from the police to investigate the *next day regrets* of some unstable marmot.

In the spring of 2016 though, my luck just about ran out. The fallout from that event has made me more leery of women than ever before.

It happened at work. Well, at least that is where it started. In 2005 I began working for a school district where I remained employed until June of 2016. For a while it was the best job I ever had. That started changing in 2012 when it quickly transformed into the worst job I ever had.

Throughout my time with the district we had a contract with an IT firm for tech support. The main agent in my building was a woman about five years younger than me. Her looks were quite striking. She was 30 at the time and always wore a huge smile. Her name was Mrs. Lollini and I will just refer to her as Mrs. L from here on out.

She was married to an Italian fellow who I never met. Mrs. L always showed interest in me from the beginning. We used to talk quite often and I enjoyed her. Mrs. L was one of the few friendly people I knew. I did notice, however, that computers were not really her thing. When serious problems arose, Mrs. L never knew what to do. She called in some guy from the home office to do the dirty work. I asked her about it once. Mrs. L had a degree in "networking systems" she reported, and was not really a techie. It did not interest her.

Every time I asked her about my computer she had little to say except "IBMs suck. Grow a pair and buy an Apple." She may have been right, but the district had provided me with a Lenovo...so that was what I used.

Soon, we found that we had similar backgrounds. We were both Michigan refugees living in Chicago. In fact, we were from neighboring Detroit suburbs. I was from Troy and she was from Sterling Heights.[26] We had much in common. It turned out that she went to the University of Michigan and her father did as well. They were both rabid fans. She loved Michigan football just as I did as a boy.

I used go to Ann Arbor between the ages of 19 and 21 to party with my friends when we were home from college. My best friend Lynch was out of control and I loved to be up there to ride along with the tiger. Many of my memories must seem bizarre to kids today. It was an open unsupervised time. We had little to worry about.

Yet my love for the Wolverines (Michigan football) never survived my encounters with actual students. They were long-leg-haired feminist "hippies" and politically correct manginas. The Social Justice Warriors spawned like cockroaches on that campus…and still do. I did not know about cultural Marxism or SJWs back then, but the place was pure poison. None of those drones thought as I did. It was Prinz Albrectstrasse to me.[27]

Regardless, both Mrs. L and I grew up hearing Bob Ufer call Michigan games on the radio. She told her father about me and he liked me from a distance. I began to notice that there was some father transference behind our interactions.

From Wikipedia, a definition of psychological transference is "the inappropriate repetition in the present of a relationship that was important in a person's childhood."[28] Soon I was even emailing her dad and the fine fellow confided to her (allegedly) that he wished, "She had married Bernard."

It got more outlandish from there.

Mrs. L and her husband had three female children. She carried them during the period in which we were coworkers. Yet after each childbirth she came back to work thinner than she was previously. It was remarkable!

Pregnancy was every woman's justification for being a heifer, but she defied the culture and its clichés by coming back slimmer than before. She was lean and hard. Her skin was as brown as a cigar which contrasted with her dyed platinum blonde mane. I used to call her "Bright White!"

Motherhood seemed to satisfy her. It appeared to me that she enjoyed every day. I admired that. Mrs. L used to send me videos of her children. I honestly had no idea why she kept doing it.

Personally, I pitied her husband. Three girls meant a lifetime of servitude. The kids were cute though and I complimented them. Mrs. L and I spoke often as we worked. It was curious though because she never seemed like she had much to do. When I asked about her wage I found out that she was being paid $40 an hour. She had a killer job!

There was something non-Kosher though about the whole interaction between us. It was always in the back of my mind. Sometimes I would catch her staring at me with maximum intensity. I did not know why. It was as if she wanted to devour me. That she was married made me think I was imagining things. Mrs. L just wanted to be my friend. Was not that the case?

Honestly, my own chamber here may be oiled but is not clean. If she did "like" me I did not discourage her. I consider myself to be a MAN of HONOR™ but nothing in this story makes me look respectable. Her family was Republican so she was nominally on the right, but for no real reason that she could explain. However, her husband was a Democrat…for no reason that he reportedly could explain.

Mrs. L used to battle her mother-in-law's bra-jerk Hillary Clinton regressivism, and often asked me for arguments. Her own political ideas were limited. Of course, I provided them. That's what I do. I am not sure if she was able to execute these arguments or not, but I disgraced myself on one occasion by telling her to "drop that leftist" after she complained about her husband. That is something I often say in various contexts, but it was wrong to say that to a married woman. In my own defense, I never thought the Lollini's relationship was fragile.

Mr. L was involved in some sort of work in the medical field for which he was well paid. They seemed happy. They were a good looking couple. Water seeks its own level and she had found hers. They owned a beautiful home in the Beverly section of Chicago where the husband was raised and had lots of social connections. They were of average intelligence (maybe).

I noted that the husband lacked all of my puffiness and water retention. He too was a lean machine. I'd imagine that a lot of women found him attractive. What bored her about him I did not know.

Mrs. L did not know too much about anything including "network systems." All she would really say is that our district connections sucked and that we should get new ones. Her conversation was very impressionistic and lacking in detail.

Once she insisted that I loan her a book I had reviewed for my channel. She said she finished it in a day and then handed it back. Mrs. L said she "loved it," but never explained why she did nor did she ever reference the work again.

She often emailed me at home concerning rumors about work. Mrs. L enjoyed the gossip but was terrified that it would one day be about her.

When everyone turned against your innocent narrator in March of 2014, Mrs. L did not speak up on my behalf but she refused to join in with the frenzied Bern-bashing. She provided me with information about who said what which allowed me to better identify my enemies. I thanked her for that. It was a lot better than anything else I got from that malignant crew.

There were no major changes in our relationship until 2014. The first time I began to wonder if something was wrong with her was over that Christmas. For no apparent reason she emailed me 200 times about my "talking about her at work." It was not true. None of her accusations had any foundation. I had no idea what she was talking about. I protested my innocence and thought she had been snorting glue.

After all, who would talk to me? It was I who they talked about. No one at work cared about my opinion concerning social dynamics. Moreover, no one ever asked me about her—not even once in 10 years.

A couple of weeks later she was back to normal. Chatting gaily about this or that and mentioning the gossip she had heard. She still did not "trust me 100 percent." Mrs. L must have thought I got turned into a sorority girl before Christmas.

Some of the ladies went out drinking after work on Fridays. Mrs. L sometimes went with them. I never attended any of these gatherings. I was seldom invited, but I also had no interest in being there. As I always used to say, "If I drank with my co-workers I would have no-workers."

My seeming lack of pride and pansy-like behaviors would be extinguished by a single shot of scotch. I am a method actor and alcohol blocks my channel to meekness. After a few drinks I would no longer find myself funny. I would *find them funny* and tell them the reasons why. Never, ever, did I drink with my co-workers.

Yet Mrs. L always tried to get me to go out. She wanted to meet me and my most excellent friend Dave on a Friday at a Hooter's in Indiana. We went twice a month or so on Fridays. We also went to the Tilted Kilt. These were breast-aurants. It was not the normal place to take a female co-worker.

Many of my teammates would look irritated when I mentioned that I frequented those places. Wasn't I too old for that? The waitresses could be my daughters, etc. Sadly, they have no idea that male sexual proclivities are timeless. I change but my fantasies do not. I did not explain that to them. Yet I definitely told them about Hooters on purpose.

Mrs. L wanted to "check it out" and go with us despite Hooters being 35 miles from where she lived. She did try to manipulate us into going out to a place by her instead. This made me laugh. I had to gently tell her that I was going to see Dave and enjoy the sights. If she went that was fine. If she didn't go that was also copacetic.

In November of 2015, she made the trip down to Indiana to see us. She had contractor hours so she got off before me. She arrived at 4 pm, but, unbeknownst to us, that franchise had closed for remodeling. Dave and I got down there an hour later and Mrs. L was long gone. We went to the Tilted Kilt instead but she had to get back to her kids.

From that point onward she kept pestering me about going out. I did not care one way or another, but she had another Christmas surprise for me. The emails flung about again alleging that she knew I was "talking about her." Whenever I asked for an explanation she would not give me one, saying, "I know, I know you did it." It was paranoid and disturbed. She would not listen to reason but instead kept accusing me of stuff. I told her I felt very sorry for her husband—a statement that inflamed her further.

Mrs. L claimed that I was being "a real ass" for not responding to her emails fast enough. Why respond at all? The girl had nothing to say. It was gibberish. There was no point in talking to her.

I asked, "if I had not suffered enough at work already without her torturing me further." Mrs. L then accused me back rather than answer any question I posed. Except for her diet, she seemed to have zero control over her life.

I found myself in the middle of psycho centrale. I told the little toolbar things like "I am a MAN of HONOR™ stop treating me like a girl." Yet it did not end until I blocked her and could no longer see what the idiot was pecking into her phone.

Mrs. L succeeded in greatly annoying me. By the end of winter break I had blocked her on Facebook and had thrown her email address into my spam filter for good measure. I am a serious man and I do not need to be wasting my time with a housewife's prattle.

I had enough. I wanted out of the sorority. I tried to avoid her as best I could for three months. Whenever she spoke I gave her the Oprah headnod. I just wanted to get away from her. I knew, at that point, there was something wrong with her personality. I was not sure what though.

I can detect depressives, obsessive-compulsives, narcissists, borderlines, and psychopaths with ease but she was not any of those. I did know, however, that I had a rattle bag on my hands. Mrs. L came up to me saying that she could tell that "something had changed. You're not acting the same."

I wasn't. It was hard to be friendly and conversational with an email bomber. She had no reservations about harassing me in my home over phantom grievances. Who the hell wants to be around someone like that?

As January moved into February and then into March, I began to forget about the danger. I had lots of enemies at work. Mrs. L was an odd duck but not an enemy. Despite her fitness, I never had much in the way of physical attraction for her. Mrs. L did not have a Bern-body. She was too thin. I did not think of her as an object of attraction.

Like Roosh in Montreal, I had come to believe that the menace had passed. Her emails petered out. I forgot how obsessive, intense, and vexing she was. I sort of forgave her. I was distracted by other forms of malignment at work. She was not so bad in light of the other things going on.

One day in March, Mrs. L said she could "hang out" with Dave and I after work. I said sure. Dave had just moved to Hammond so we planned on going to Three Floyds Brewery. Dave cancelled though at the last minute so I was left alone with Mrs. L. I did not think anything of it, but the tint on my frame was getting darker.

Earlier in the day, Mrs. L saw me talking in the hallway to an enterprising youth named Smith. We were talking about students. Mrs. L came up to me at lunch and said, "Does Mr. Smith know we're going out?"

"What? *Going out*? I thought we were just have a drink after work. What are you talking about?"

She nodded and told me not to tell anyone including Mr. Smith.

I was a bit addled but went through with it. I had already talked to Mr. Smith about her though. He had suggested to me a place about nine miles away because Three Floyds would be mobbed. I took his word on it. We changed destinations. We went there but not without incident. She didn't want to use her GPS, instead she wanted to "follow me." Mrs. L called my cell phone several times to prevent me from "losing her."

Eventually we arrived at the sports bar. I planned on having two drinks. That was the norm for such circumstances. I went heavy and ordered a Three Floyd's ale called "Yum Yum." It was 5.5% alcohol but two would do me little harm in terms of impairment. Unfortunately, Mrs. L ordered the same thing which I did not like due to her lack of body fat. I made no comment though.

I ordered food which she then proceeded to make fun of due to its unhealthy content. For her part, she ate nothing. With each passing five minute span she got goofier and goofier…and more outrageous!

Rather than sit across from me she sat at a seat on my right shoulder. Mrs. L said this was "our first date." She asked if people "were looking at her" due to her wedding ring.

I said, "No, why would they be looking at you?" I had no idea what she was babbling about. Weren't we just going out after work? Isn't that what people do? From there it got bizarre.

The middle aged waitress was completely freaked out by her. The server proved a good judge of character. Mrs. L was very loud and everyone started looking over at our table. I became uncomfortable. I would rather have been at work which is really saying something.

Mrs. L had no reserve. Her volume level startled me. Her mouth was a Bose speaker. I wanted to flee. This was about as relaxing as doing wind sprints.

I regard myself as being mentally quick but I was not on that day. Gradually, I began to realize that Mrs. L had a gigantic and dramatic agenda for this meeting. I was about to be a major star in her production.

Why didn't I see it coming? All the emails, the perpetual concerns about "people talking about her," and the longing of her stare should have told me I had drove into a trap. I felt sorry for her. That was misdirected. I should have felt sorry for myself.

Mrs. L kept drinking and drinking. She ordered a third beer. I told the waitress I did not want another. The waitress brought two anyway. I glared at her. Who taught you how to treat customers? I did not drink more than a third of it.

Soon Mrs. L was practically yelling in the bar and acting like a buffoon. I saw a thin man in his fifties (perhaps a MGTOW ambassador) at the next table who was blatantly cracking up over her antics. He sat alone and loved the entertainment. It was really a show. You can see the headline on the theatre bill— DISTURBED FEMALE TORMENTS MAN—but I was not amused. I just wanted to get the hell out of there.

Then Mrs. L ordered a fourth beer. I refused to quaff any more from my third. I told the waitress not to bring it for her but she did anyway. I stood up and approached the waitress and handed her my credit card. Finally, she followed instructions. She took the bill, ran it through the machine, and the night should have been over. This peeved Mrs. L. She hounded the poor server crying, "No, no, no, no, I'm paying for this. I'm paying for this. Give me that check."

"Mrs. L," I said. "It's over with. She's charged my account already."

"Wrong, delete his charge and put mine through. That's final. You have to do that!" Isn't that the craziest thing you've ever heard?

The waitress was horrified and so was I. The MGTOW guy was on his phone probably trying to encourage other lads to drive over so they could witness the spectacle.

The employee tried to argue, but Mrs. L was out of her chair acting a fool. The server reluctantly deleted my charge and replaced it with hers.

I stood up and put on my coat. "This is horrible. Your behavior is disgraceful."

Mrs. L turned to me. "You owe me 30 dollars."

"I do not."

"You do. Your half is 30 dollars."

"How do you know she did not just charge both of our credit cards?"

"She didn't. Give me 30."

I stood up and handed the waitress ten bucks for having to put up with all of this. Then I gave Mrs. L $20. "We'll wait to see what is on my card tomorrow."[29]

Mrs. L kept drinking. She announced, "I'm drunk. I don't know how I'm going to get home."

This statement hit me hard. I could not hold back my bile. "You're fucking 40 years old and you don't how much liquor you can hold? You're not 21. What the fuck!"

"You got me drunk!" She bellowed. Then she began laughing hysterically.

Everyone was looking at me. I felt like a rodeo clown. I stood up again. "I'm leaving."

"Not without me you aren't!" She followed but I disappeared into the bathroom. When I was done with the urinal Mrs. L was standing in front of me outside the door. "Now you have to wait for me to go to the bathroom too. I don't want to walk to the car alone."

Looking back on the incident, this was the only moment in which I could have avoided the disaster that followed. What I should have done is waited for her to shut the door and then ran off. Yet I had no idea about the stunt she was about to pull. The full parameters of her agenda were unknown.

We walked to our cars. I put the key in my door. She got on the other side. "I'm too drunk to drive. Let me sit in your car for a while to sober up."

This was the moment wherein I relinquished control over the situation. I did as she asked. She sat in the car and refused to get out. I should have pulled out my phone and began taking a video. That probably would have worked. She was terrified of what people thought. Mrs. L feared their "talking about her" enough where that may have got her out of the Carolla. I could have uploaded it and been a WorldStarHipHop hero like our friend, Marcus A. Brown…but sadly I did not think of it.

She kept hitting the driver's side seat and telling me to jump in. Reluctantly, I did so. Mrs. L started doing the Brutus/Olive Oil routine with me, asking for one kiss, "just one kiss." I kissed her and then it started. We were making out in the car like a couple of high school kids. Her body felt very hard.

I then resisted. I told she had to go home now. I got out of the car. She still refused to leave. I began pleading with her. I was practically begging her. Mrs. L was acting like a three-year-old. My gut told me to grab her by the arm and yank her out of the car. This would have been a very bad decision. There were all sorts of cops around. I had drank over two heavy beers. I was fine but what would I blow if arrested? I could have got a DUI along with battery charges.

I whined like a Schweizer. I said, "Come on, Mrs. Lollini, please get out of my car. What the heck? I have now asked you five times."

"No, I'm too drunk to drive. You have to take care of me."

"Take care of you? You're a fucking adult!"

I was wrong. That was no adult. I was dealing with an infant. I should have been able to see that this individual had no boundaries whatsoever. She freely disregarded my wishes. I would never treat another person like that. I need to remember that people like me are an exception in this world.

Homo homini lupus. Man is a wolf to man. Those are the words that you need to internalize to understand the world and the single man's place in it. "Treat people well and they'll treat you well" is a fantasy. Even though I try to practice it every day.

I waited for five minutes and got back in my car. It felt like it had been possessed. She leaned over and we began kissing. I felt her. Lean and taut. I had not touched something like that in two years.

"Feel my boobs," she said. "You won't believe how big they are and firm." I did. She was right. I blame what followed partially on the obesity epidemic. Honestly I do. Had I the opportunity to date women regularly who were not in the BTB range the night may have had a different outcome.

Mrs. L then began shouting. "Take me to your house! Take me to your house! I want to see it…that shack!"

I said no for about five minutes. My house was 16 miles away. Then I would have to drive back there afterwards in the middle of the night. I did not want anything to do with this malarkey. Yet…we left. I was attracted to her body. She was cottage cheese free. I felt like someone who had not drunk water for three days and was suddenly given a gallon of it. I knew it was wrong though. This was going to be serious trouble. I had second thoughts when saw a White Castle on the side of the road. I offered to go into it and buy her some coffee so she could sober up.

"I'm not going to a fucking White Castle! Just drive."

She left off, "you peasant," but I was definitely the peasant in the scenario.

On the way my unconscious understood that this girl was very unstable. I needed help. I started calling guys that I knew for insurance. She cooperated by babbling into the phone talking about how lucky I was about to get her. They heard her on the voice mails the next day. I called Dave, no answer. I left a message. I then did the same thing with Yakov. Mrs. L warbled into their recorders.

When we got to my house I had bad trepidations about going inside. The place was a mess as it usually is on Fridays. I only clean on Sundays. My dress shirts were draped over chairs waiting to be rehung. What was worse was that I had not vacuumed. The significance of that will be evident momentarily.

I got out a diet soda and offered one to Mrs. L. No good. She wanted to keep drinking. I said no. After five minutes she got her way, I opened a warm Guinness for her. I put it in a cup. She sprawled out on my couch setting the beer down on the carpet. Mrs. L then called me over there to kiss her. I did so kicking the Guinness over in the process. I turned on the lights and began cleaning it up.

She saw my copy of Matt Forney's autographed *Big Lovin': The Guide to Picking Up Fat Chicks*. "What the hell is this?" She demanded. The conspiratorial nature of her mind was evident in her expressed conclusion. I was its writer! I had written it under the pseudonym of Matt Forney. That was my book, wasn't it?

I said, "No, Matt Forney is a real person. As a matter of fact let's call him on the phone." I needed more witnesses. Part of me felt she was going to portray the night radically different from how it was.

I handed her the phone. She told Forney about "how lucky" I was getting with her and about what a good time we were having. Mrs. L then gave the phone back to me. Rather than ask about the android he had just spoken to, Forney told me about the cancelled Trump rally and about that night's events in Chicago. I hung up the phone and wished that it was Forney in my house instead of me. I wanted out.

Moments later we went into the bedroom and that action lasted for about a half hour. I will spare you the details. Let me just state that I remained fully clothed the whole time. Part of me was disgusted that I had a married woman in my bed, and the other part was very impressed with her torso. I do not regard myself as being the sort of guy who does those things. I'm better than that. Only I wasn't. I would have actually enjoyed it if she had a functional personality. Wishful thinking.

Then I put on my boots and told her it was time to go. Mrs. L howled, "Hell no! I'm sleeping over. The night is still young!"

I tried reasoning with her. No one stays out late after work and her husband would be looking for her. It was time to go. Blah, blah, blah…

I stood there in the doorway begging her to leave. She kept saying she was drunk, but I noticed that now she was talking the same way she always did at work. Mrs. L sounded completely normal. She was no stranger to alcohol.

After another 30 minutes, I got her out the door at 10:25. I had finished four diet root beers and felt safe to drive. When she got out of the car at the sports bar I was greatly relieved. Was the worst of the ordeal over?

Mrs. L began texting me that night telling me about what an awesome time we had and that we should "do it again." A week passed by and then she started to change. She quickly turned on me. Why was I ignoring her? I told her I did not want to have a relationship with a married woman and that was that. She said she missed talking to me and that she valued my "friendship." Oh God!

Two weeks later, at closing time, she cornered me in my office. Mrs. L was her loud self. She did not want people talking about her but was practically shouting out our business. Mrs. L claimed to "not know how to process what happened." She said, "I need to talk to you about this. Where do we go from here?"

"Look, you're at work," I answered. "This is not the place for this. Call me at home." We both knew I wouldn't be answering the phone though. I got my bag but she followed me out to my car. I had to shut the door in her face in order to escape. She started giving me dirty looks at work thereafter. Fine, anything to be done with her. But was I done?

A month later, after swearing that she would not tell her husband, she emailed me to say that they had talked and he "was fine with it."

I did not reply. I put her address back into the spam filter. I wanted to exit this carnival permanently. Mrs. L continued to send me emails at work and videos of her daughters. I ignored all of them. Two months later, the scary stuff began.

On a hunch, one Sunday in May, I checked my spam filter. There she was! I got an email reading "PS...my husband knows what those pills are...you fricking asshole." This was followed with, "MY LAWYER WILL BE CONTACTING YOU, DON'T WORRY. YOU WONT HEAR FROM ME AGAIN."

I had no idea what she was talking about. Mrs. L had finally succeeded in discovering a way to get me to acknowledge and respond to her messages.

I tried for several emails to get to what she was alleging. By the end of the afternoon it became clear that she had noticed a pill on the ground when I was cleaning up the spilled Guinness. In a crazy person's mind this could only mean one thing! I was trying to drug her.

Using toddler calculus, she figured that the pill had come from the beer. Never mind that it was not dissolved and that it still looked like it came from the container. Never mind that the place was a mess and I had not vacuumed in two weeks. Never mind that I have no children so I do not have to be concerned about what falls to the ground.

I told her that the pill—I assume an expensive Imitrex for migraines that I had to subsequently throw out—probably fell from my table. So what?

She responded, "I HAVE A PICTURE BERNARD.... YOU SPILLED THE BLACK DRINK WITH TWO HALF PILLS......... STOP LYING."

I knew I was dealing with a total psycho now. This was a succubus. All my life I had received messages from guys with links or their own stories about similar plots and now it was happening to me. I was going to be the new guy pleading for help on an MRA comment board. It was my turn. An innocent man framed. I was about to be prosecuted, and for what exactly? I did not know as we did not have sex. Yet losing my freedom is my number one fear in life as it is for most libertarians.

I spoke to my mother about it. Mrs. L's dysfunction was easily diagnosed. My mother was a clinical psychologist for 30 years. She had her own private practice that dealt exclusively with neurotic career girls. Mom knows women inside and out. Mrs. L was obvious for her.

My mother was convinced that Mrs. L had put on this Manson-esque proceeding two months after the incident in the hopes of capturing the sympathy of her husband. That was her new audience. He may have been wondering what he was doing with her. She may have been obsessing/worrying over his possible departure from her life as well. Perhaps acting as if she was drugged would make things alright with him.

I finally got her to stop bothering me by emailing, "Why would I have needed to drug you? I couldn't get rid of you. You wouldn't get out of my car or my home. You were totally receptive. It was I who said no."

I think she was showing her husband the messages previously and concluded this was probably a bad one to share. I never heard from this mysterious lawyer. I never did see "the picture" nor did I ever hear explained how taking a non-existent pill at 9:30 pm would account for all of her bats in the belfry behaviors between 4:30 and 9:30. There could be no answers.

She was another unbalanced woman who tormented me unnecessarily. I seem to be a magnet. Where would it end?

It ends with **MGTOW FOREVER**. I cannot handle these people anymore, and I do not want anything to do with them. Inside, I'm as disappointed and burnt out on the opposite sex as any of the guys you see posting comments on Youtube channels like Sandman's.

To this day Mrs. L still emails me. I find her messages in my spam filter every so often. I blocked her on Twitter, Facebook, Google+, Soundcloud, and finally on Youtube. That she posted on Youtube was more evidence of instability as I look like Bishop Tutu when compared to my subscribers. I am a warm cushiony pillow of radiating warmth when placed alongside them. They would carve her into tofu. Yet she still strives to get my attention.

That I did not have sex with her was the best decision I ever made.

Romantically, I operate under the bylaw "there's you, there's me, there's us." More and more I have come to notice that with the ornate sex, it's just "her." No thanks. I have no interest in spending the rest of my life as the sorceresses' apprentice. Freedom over Maledom.

In MGTOW, there is a saying: "Better a monk than a slave." Brother Bernard reporting for Vespers.

10. Conclusion: No Surrender!

Some cause happiness wherever they go; others whenever they go.
—Oscar Wilde

In *The Wrestler*, the main character gives a speech shortly before his (presumed) death. Addressing the audience before his final match. His last words are:

> *You know what? The only one that's going to tell me*
> *when I'm through doing my thing is you people here.*
> *You people here —You people here are the ones who*
> *are worth bringing it for because you're my family.*

That sums up my current condition. The film exhilarated but also disturbed. His character still haunts me. About a week after I saw it I knew it was somewhere on my favorite's list. Upon seeing it a second time, *The Wrestler* immediately catapulted itself over *The Lord of the Rings* and *A Room with a View* into the number one position on my favorite film list.

That it impressed me so was partially subjective. Yes, it's an excellent movie, of that there is no doubt, but I view the Mickey Rourke classic as being completely biographical…biographical of me. It has implicit meaning in the context of my life.

The situation in which the main character, Robin "The Ram" Ramzinski, finds himself during the action is very much akin to my own.

Like the Ram, physically I have seen better days. I'm over the hill. I cannot work out for all the hours that I used to even when I have the time. It's been since 2000 when I could put 335 pounds up on the bench press. After knee surgery in 2007, I have not ran more than 10 yards at a clip. I too, often feel like a "broken down piece of meat."

Another similarity is that most of my romantic relationships have been failures. Well, I certainly enjoyed them or at least *parts* of them, but I remain very much alone in this world. By choice I'm not on speaking terms with my exes and have no desire for that situation to change. The world can have them! Yet, except for sheer numbers, romantically, I am a non-achiever.

Robin appears to be lonely. I am not, but old drives and desires are tough to break. I'm in Females Anonymous for a reason.

I have no wish for anyone to take care of me in any capacity, but I cannot deny the pleasure of having a woman on a steady basis. It's something I do miss. Placing someone that you love and trust on your arm is a powerful feeling, but most of the times that I experienced those feelings they dissipated quickly. It often turned out that my trust was displaced. Our "love" did not endure.

Merely "finding a woman" is not much of an obstacle. As I mentioned in a previous chapter, most of the ones I can get are my age…which is far from optimal. Further, they often are single mothers who are morbidly obese. I want nothing to do with that demographic. While it's true that I have the firepower in my home to bring down a moose, I certainly don't want to copulate with one. Being with them would not satisfy.

Ultimately, it does not matter. I don't care if I "find someone" ever again. If nothing comes my way for the next 30 years then that's that. I'm going my own way. I will still be here. Living solo is an end in itself. Every day that I am home I am free. It is never boring to me. Being paid to write all day fulfills my greatest dreams.

In the film, the Ram is a failure at making money outside of the ring. Over an affront to his pride, he goes ballistic and quits the one side job that he has. He has no prospects at all as he cannot wrestle anymore.

That certainly isn't true for me. For 21 years, I have had all the financial security I needed. That period has now ended. Yes, I face a cold and hungry future, but I believe that I will excel and make it.

As a person, I have few demands. The ones I possess are currently met. I have food, shelter, and health. It is natural to always want more, but I appreciate my ramshackle home. My car is reliable and mostly paid off. I have no reason to complain. I'm not living in a tent and this is no Bergen-Belsen.

As far as being a school psychologist goes, I certainly have not been "a success" by the common definition. I never won any awards, and about the best compliment I ever received was from a former student a couple of months ago. He came back to visit the junior high and saw me in the hallway. He excitedly pointed at me. The lad said, "There's the guy that helped me pass 8th grade!" What better thing to hear?

After 21 years I was put up for termination by the superintendent due to a conspiracy orchestrated by a throng of gossipy Neanderthals who despise labor. The proposal was countermanded by the board. Yet the conspirators were my "co-workers." Only they don't go to work to work. They go there to fuck with people. They are empty and pathetic. The whole nefarious story will be told in the near future. For them, it was easier to critique my Youtube channel than to simply teach kids. They were opposed to such activities as it cut down on their female verbal companionship time.

If the particular school which gave me the most trouble were to suddenly alter its gender skew, I have no doubt that many of them would resign. Without their in-group affiliation and daily victimhood affirmation they would probably need 24/7 therapy.

C'est la vie. It may be a cliché but this book is an act of love. My graduate degree allowed me to lead a middle class existence for two decades which is better than many have it. I knew a former reader who graduated from a school psychology program but dropped out of the field after a single year. He went into sales. He admired me for putting up with all of it. I don't. I wish I had broken out sooner.

I went into my field blind. I applied to a graduate school and finished two years later. Then I got a job. Technically, it all worked out. I never thought much about the career that followed. It just happened. If I had it to do over again I would have gone into finance, but it's too late for that now.

Besides, it turned out that I was naturally good at working with children. The parents were rarely a problem. I always volunteered whatever time I had to help their sons and daughters. They knew I was a sympathetic figure rather than simply a dumb bureaucrat. There's about ten kids I will think about in the near future, and I feel like I let them down. Yet it was not my choice to leave.

My choice was free speech or getting harassed by defective females for 15 more years. The decision was an easy one. I accept my circumstances. Downward mobility is a small price to pay for liberty and never being chained to braindead affirmative action manikins again.

Working in my profession though should not have been as daunting as it was. On paper, it still seems a groovy sort of gig. I loved working with the population. I find human behavior inherently fascinating. The mental aspects of the profession were always enjoyable. So, what was the problem?

It was structural. Within my greater profession, 87 percent[30] of the employees are women. Within my specific field, the percentage of females is 77 percent.[31] Recall what I discovered in 2002, "I just don't get along with these people." The outcome was predictable. I mind my own business which is an affront to them. It is very difficult for a guy like me to produce when he is surrounded by individuals who despise production. Yet produce I did anyway.

Gender ratios are nothing I cared to research when I was 22. Even if I would have, it would not have bothered me. I knew none of the things I know now. I probably would have screamed "Babe-o-Rama" upon hearing that I would be surrounded by women. I figured they would act just like guys. I mean, right? On the job women would be just like men but more attractive.

No, my ignorance was colossal.

I prefer work over talk. Only a handful of my female peers agreed. Moreover, I always act. I make decisions. What I never do is ask 25 people (except my supervisor) for what to do, and then decide that no effort is the best course of action.

This partially explains the many difficulties I had in my profession. I always appeared conspicuously hard-working which caused resentment. The only thing I had going for me intuitively at age 25 was that I was smart enough never to eat with them in the teacher's lounge. Had I done so, our tremendous dissimilarities would have become blatantly evident.

Lastly, one of the side effects from my years of working alongside women and from dating them is that I have developed a major allergy to passive aggressive conduct. I suffered from full-immersion in the female culture. I understand them all too well. I comprehend passive-aggressive perfectly, but I refuse to speak it. *The language of Mordor will not be uttered here!*

At one point, I counted seven personality disorders within my place of work; all of them present within female employees. They collided with everyone who either paid attention to them or ignored them. You could not win.

I recall that the one who was a psychopathic narcissist made the malignant narcissists look like Bambi. Narcissism produces intense jealousy. The goal of the narcissist on the job is to prevent others from doing anything. When no one is effective they look less like a cancer in the organization. What they crave are endless meetings with female peers whose results can best be described with the acronym FUBAR. I was a work completer, and, thus, a mortal enemy.

As a man—and one advanced in years—I have a highly developed sense of honor. My word is my bond. When I say something I mean it. My word is your receipt. This characteristic clashed mightily with the personalities exhibited by my peers. Many of them preferred being ceaselessly irresponsible and always blaming someone else for the mistakes that they made. They were practitioners of Nearest Male Doctrine, and were quick to critique and blame a man for whatever they failed to do.

All of these obstacles within my vocation made every day there uncertain and often unpleasant. I thought to myself, as Robin undoubtedly did in the film, I can't go on. Certainly no monuments will be built for me by the other practitioners of my trade.

The only place the Ram excels is in the ring. Writing and making videos is my version of the ring. When I turn on my video camera or recorder I am instantly in an outstanding mood. I feel as if I am doing what God wants me to do. Exercising my talent, however limited it may be, fills me with joy.

Most of my supporters are atheists. I respect their diversity, but without God I would be a far less content person. I believe God put me on this earth to defend western civilization. I believe that our civilization is in massive jeopardy. I am here to speak out. I argue and proclaim on the behalf of those who cannot or will not do so.

The majority say nothing. The world happens to them. Most of those who take a stand use fake names and manufactured IDs on the internet. They are smart. They don't want to be associated with politically incorrect ideas out of fear for their jobs or who knows what. They are right to take this approach. To make the truth known at present can result in a life ruined. You should not be like me.

PC is utter hogwash. It's psychobabble, and, as we know, psychos love to babble. There is no reason for us to bow before these draconian despots…ever. So, I fight, even if I have to fight alone. Every time I do so it fills me with purpose. Each click on the microphone or clack on the keyboard reminds me that I am doing what I was born to do. It's a unique and mighty feeling. Ram had his tights and his Ram-Jam[32]…I have my keyboard.

With little long-term romantic success and a great deal of *sturm und drang* at the end of my daily commute for 21 years, one starts to wonder what exact successes I have had. How am I different from the Ram? The answer is all of you.

Recall his last words:

> *You people here – You people here are the ones who are worth bringing it for because you're my family.*

While my readers/viewers are not technically my family, I get along with them a lot better than I do my actual relatives. My supporters are intrinsic to my contentment.

Like the stumbling mountain Mickey Rourke plays, I am a relic. My kind are leaving these shores, and each day the press takes great pride in announcing that our future in North America is endangered. The fate for people like me is that we're not supposed to have a future. I do not choose to believe this. Every day I put my trust in Providence. Fuck the media. Fuck our bureaucrats. Fuck the left.

Let's win this thing!

Randy the Ram risks his life to wrestle once more. He points to the rest of the world and concludes, "The only place I get hurt is out there." That was true for almost all of his days. So far, it's definitely been true of mine.

Sometimes the only fun I have is when I go to the gym and/or make a video and write. Based on my past history of physical and romantic injuries though, I can safely say that the only place I don't get hurt is here in the intellectual sphere.

The online arena is one for which I am uniquely suited. Nobody depresses me or makes me question myself. I have an old school approach to self-esteem. At 46, my self-concept is concrete and no one can alter it. I do not care what they say. Nothing and no one gets me down. I am self-aware. No opponent can deter my performance. I will march forward in spite of their kitty-cattery. I know who I am.

My weaknesses and strengths are evident. The same cannot be said for my foes, however. They are delusionac derelicts who have to call online support every time someone slurs in their direction. Our opponents are pussies and cowards. Whatever insults they give I shall return. I call that social justice.

Here, I am king…and only here. Elsewhere I am a serf. To women, I am part of the vast male blur. The only place I stand out is in print or video. I will keep standing out. I am in this struggle for the duration. There will be no surrender. No surrender!

Aaron Clarey encouraged his readers to *Enjoy the Decline*. I will not do the same. I don't appreciate witnessing the greatest nation on earth dissolve into an acid bath of cultural Marxism and masochism. The Donald Trump run for the presidency gives me massive hope. Win or lose he awoke those who were ready to quit. Our minds are free. Our quest for liberty will never die.

I wrote this book for you. I'll only be done "doing my thing" when *you people here* say so. Capitulation is not an option. We can defeat our foes. Let's parry their blows until victory or death. I'll never stop. I have your back.

Bernard Chapin
Indiana, USA
July, 2016

[1] Technically, "Men Going Their Own Way."

[2] I will use cultural Marxism and synonyms interchangeably.

[3] *Muffington Boast*, "Lauren Hutton Slams "Sex And The City" Writers: "Guys Who Are Sluts." Here's the link: http://www.huffingtonpost.com/2008/05/29/lauren-hutton-slams-sex-a_n_104195.html

[4] *Eonline.com*, "Jon Cryer's Ex-Wife Asking for $88,969 per Month in Child Support!" Here's the link: http://www.eonline.com/news/474417/jon-cryer-s-ex-wife-asking-for-88-969-per-month-in-child-support-find-out-why

[5] Nationalparentsorgantion.org. "TV Star Jon Cryer Must Pay Child Support For Son In His Custody." Here is the link: https://nationalparentsorganization.org/blog/18741-tv-star-jon-cryer-mu

[6] *UK Daily Mail*. "Businesswoman who dumped her career to become 'conventional housewife' has last laugh on her high flying ex when divorce judge awards her ALL their £500,000 fortune." Here is the link: http://www.dailymail.co.uk/news/article-3491641/Businesswoman-dumped-career-conventional-housewife-laugh-high-flying-ex-divorce-judge-awards-500-000-fortune.html

[7] The advertising slogan of Virginia Slims cigarettes back in the 1980s when I was a wee lad.

[8] LOL

[9] I got that argument from Roosh V.

[10] If they did know my name I would then pretend that I did not hear them lol.

[11] Can you believe how embarrassing this story is?

[12] The Buzzy's mother basically threw the guy out for trying to discipline the kids. That's what was reported to me anyway.

[13] Drops cap, Detroit Red Wings

[14] Between 77 and 80 percent of school psychologists are female. Here's the link: https://www.questia.com/library/journal/1G1-351434712/gender-and-race-in-school-psychology

[15] I could not find his name or the quote online. For the record, I did not come up with that on my own.

[16] That's a quote by Henry Ford in relation to the Model T.

[17] "Overweight, obesity, and weight loss fact sheet." *Womenshealth.gov*. Here is the link: http://www.womenshealth.gov/publications/our-publications/fact-sheet/overweight-weight-loss.html

[18] "40 Percent of US Women are Now Obese." *Time.com*. June 7th 2016. Here is the link: http://time.com/4359637/obesity-americans-women-men/

[19] Hat tip to Roger Kimball. *Against the Idols of the Age* was a great book.

[20] Guidetopsychology.com "Boundaries." Here is the link: http://www.guidetopsychology.com/boundaries.htm

[21] How could I write a book without a Lord of the Rings reference?

[22] AZQuotes.com. Here is the link: http://www.azquotes.com/quote/584200

[23] AttractionInstitute.com defines shit tests as "her way of finding out whether or not you're a remarkable Man." Here's the link: http://attractioninstitute.com/pass-shit-tests/

[24] Dude, I'm totally serious. That's what it said. LOL.

[25] Their feces is actually toxic. The raccoon roundworm, *Baylisascaris,* can kill. See this CDC link: http://www.cdc.gov/parasites/baylisascaris/

[26] We used to call Sterling Heights "Sterile Whites."

[27] Home of the GESTAPO.

[28] Here is the link: https://en.wikipedia.org/wiki/Transference

[29] The waitress did delete my end of the charges.

[30] "Percentage of Teachers in Primary Education Who Are Female." *Worldbank.org* Here is the link: http://data.worldbank.org/indicator/SE.PRM.TCHR.FE.ZS

[31] "Gender and Race in School Psychology." *School Psychology Review*. Here is the link: https://www.questia.com/library/journal/1G1-351434712/gender-and-race-in-school-psychology

[32] When Rourke would fly out and bust up his adversaries with a flying elbow.

CPSIA information can be obtained
at www.ICGtesting.com
Printed in the USA
LVHW02s1349181217
560167LV00017B/561/P